T0360464

Absolute Essentials of Advertising

'A useful revision guide or overview of the area of advertising. As a text it is logically structured and takes the reader through the timeline of advertising bringing them up to date with examples of current challenges and issues encountered in the contemporary communications environment.'

Lynn McBain, *Senior Lecturer in Marketing, Oxford Brookes University, United Kingdom*

This concise textbook provides a comprehensive and clear overview of advertising theory and practice. Each chapter covers the essential aspects of the subject matter, provides a supplement for teaching and acts as a valuable revision guide. Split over three core parts, the book begins with a consideration of the role and function of advertising, the customer journey, advertising theory, planning and strategy, and moves on to the creative development process, media planning and strategy. The final chapter considers the industry as a whole and the reality of practice, outlining roles within agencies to highlight employability opportunities to students. To aid learning, each chapter contains brief real-life examples and includes questions to encourage the reader to consider how practical examples can be applied. Written by a renowned textbook author, this short-form textbook is suitable for students at all levels studying advertising. For undergraduates, the book provides a valuable support for traditional or blended online teaching. For postgraduate and MBA students, as well as those studying for professional qualifications, the book also provides a valuable resource.

Sarah Turnbull is a Reader in Advertising at the University of Portsmouth, UK.

Absolute Essentials of Business and Economics

Textbooks are an extraordinarily useful tool for students and teachers, as is demonstrated by their continued use in the classroom and online. Successful textbooks run into multiple editions, and in endeavouring to keep up with developments in the field, it can be difficult to avoid increasing length and complexity.

This series of Shortform textbooks offers a range of books which zero-in on the absolute essentials. In focusing on only the core elements of each sub-discipline, the books provide a useful alternative or supplement to traditional textbooks.

Absolute Essentials of Business Behavioural Ethics
Nina Seppala

Absolute Essentials of Corporate Governance
Stephen Bloomfield

Absolute Essentials of Business Ethics
Peter A. Stanwick & Sarah D. Stanwick

Absolute Essentials of Creative Thinking and Problem Solving
Tony Proctor

Absolute Essentials of Environmental Economics
Barry C. Field

Absolute Essentials of Marketing Research
Bonita M. Kolb

Absolute Essentials of Advertising
Sarah Turnbull

For more information about this series, please visit: www.routledge.com/ Absolute-Essentials-of-Business-and-Economics/book-series/ABSOLUTE

Absolute Essentials of Advertising

Sarah Turnbull

Routledge
Taylor & Francis Group

LONDON AND NEW YORK

First published 2022
by Routledge
4 Park Square, Milton Park, Abingdon, Oxon OX14 4RN

and by Routledge
605 Third Avenue, New York, NY 10158

*Routledge is an imprint of the Taylor & Francis Group,
an informa business*

British Library Cataloguing-in-Publication Data
A catalogue record for this book is available from the British Library

Library of Congress Cataloging-in-Publication Data
Names: Turnbull, Sarah, Dr., author.
Title: Absolute essentials of advertising / Sarah Turnbull.
Description: 1 Edition. | New York, NY : Routledge, 2022. |
   Series: Absolute essentials of business and economics |
   Includes bibliographical references and index. |
Identifiers: LCCN 2022000870 | ISBN 9781032007663 (hardback) |
   ISBN 9781032007687 (paperback) | ISBN 9781003175551 (ebook)
Subjects: LCSH: Advertising. | Strategic planning. | Internet advertising.
Classification: LCC HF5823 .T87 2022 | DDC 659.1—dc23/eng/
   20220107
LC record available at https://lccn.loc.gov/2022000870

ISBN: 978-1-032-00766-3 (hbk)
ISBN: 978-1-032-00768-7 (pbk)
ISBN: 978-1-003-17555-1 (ebk)

DOI: 10.4324/9781003175551

Typeset in Times New Roman
by Apex CoVantage, LLC

For Mum and Don . . . who set me on the advertising career path. And for Simon, Daisy and Bea . . . who are always there to support me.

Contents

Foreword

This short-form textbook provides readers with a concise overview of the fundamentals of advertising. The ten chapters cover the core aspects of the subject such as planning and strategy, advertising theory, advertising appeals, the creative development process, international advertising, media, media planning, measurement and metrics and industry structure and practice. Each chapter provides suggestions for extended reading on each topic.

The author, Sarah Turnbull, is a Reader in Advertising at the University of Portsmouth. She is co-author of *Marketing Communications: discovery, creation and conversations* (2016) and *Marketing Communications: touchpoints, sharing and disruption* (2019). Sarah is the Associate Editor for the *Journal of Marketing Management* and is a member of the Editorial Review Board of the *International Journal of Advertising* and the *Journal of Advertising Education*. She has published over 70 papers, books, articles and cases and is a Fellow of the Chartered Institute of Marketing and a Freeman of the Worshipful Company of Marketors. Sarah has an advertising agency background and led the Emirates account in Dubai for eight years. Sarah has published her research in leading international journals such as *Marketing Theory, International Journal of Small Business, International Journal of Research in Marketing, Journal of Marketing Management, International Journal of Advertising* and *Journal of Business Research.*

1   Advertising

Learning outcomes

This chapter aims to enable readers to:

1   Understand the nature and role of advertising
2   Examine the differ types of advertising
3   Appreciate the influence of advertising on society
4   Understand the role of advertising in the economy
5   Consider further reading on advertising issues highlighted

Advertising

Advertising has been practiced for centuries. The advertising on the painted walls of Pompeii dating from 79 BC is still visible to visitors and provides evidence of the importance of advertising as far back as Roman times. The History of Advertising Trust (2013) suggests that advertising can be traced back even further to around 2000 BC when Egyptians carved their public announcements on stone slabs or *stelae*. Today, advertising remains an omnipresent part of our everyday lives and continues to play a significant role in shaping politics, culture and society.

Turnbull (2019) argues that advertising is part of national culture and suggests,

> "the UK is a nation of "ad lovers." Advertising is part of the national conversation: it is discussed in the national media and school playgrounds, and is embedded within our popular culture. Even the start of Christmas in the UK has been defined by advertising, with media and consumers alike eagerly anticipating the arrival of the annual John Lewis Christmas TV ad".
>
> Turnbull (2019, p. 142)

DOI: 10.4324/9781003175551-1

In the United States, advertising for the Super Bowl is similarly seen as a "unique phenomenon" and studies have identified that seven percent of Super Bowl viewers watch the Super Bowl to see the advertising (Tomkovick et al., 2001), highlighting the cultural relevance of advertising.

While there is widespread recognition of the cultural influence of advertising, there is no universally agreed definition of what advertising is. Richards and Curran (2002, p. 74) offer a definition that has been used widely which identifies advertising as, "a paid, mediated form of communication from an identifiable source, designed to persuade the receiver to take some action, now or in the future". There has been much debate around the definition over the last decade, especially in relation to whether advertising is always "paid" for, and is likely to continue for the next decade as advertising is transformed by new media platforms and new types of advertising emerge. More recently, Jeremy Bullmore, an advisory board member for the agency holding group WPP, provided an updated definition of advertising as, "Any communication, usually paid-for, specifically intended to inform and/or influence one or more people" (2021, p. 1). The advantage of this definition is that it addresses the issue of media payment and comes from a highly respected industry practitioner.

While definitions of advertising are regularly debated, the one aspect of advertising that remains constant is the belief and understanding that advertising has the ability to influence large audiences and change consumer behaviours.

Types of advertising

Advertising is used by companies, charities, educational institutions and governments to communicate with a range of audiences, including customers, employees, stakeholders and shareholders. This has led to the emergence of a number of different types of advertising, including:

- Brand
- Business-to-business (B2B)
- Corporate
- Co-operative
- Recruitment
- Public service announcements (PSAs)
- Political
- Consumer-generated
- Brand activism
- Brand purpose
- Femvertising

Brand advertising is one of the most familiar forms of advertising and consumers are exposed to hundreds of brand messages every day. This may be to raise awareness of a new product or service, or to encourage product trial. Brands may also wish to reposition themselves in the marketplace or change consumers' attitudes to the brand. Similarly, *business-to-business (B2B) advertising* allows B2B products and services to communicate with their customers. For example, Emirates Sky Cargo may wish to raise awareness of new destinations with cargo agents or announce additional services to their customers.

Organisations also run *corporate advertising* which is usually less brand orientated and more focussed on building goodwill and relationships. For example, Proctor & Gamble (P&G) ran a corporate advertising campaign to coincide with the Olympic games in celebration of the role and support of mums. In their first-ever corporate campaign, P&G moved away from their usual brand advertising and developed a corporate campaign, "Thank You, Mom" which ran globally (Wieden + Kennedy, 2010).

Co-operative advertising is often seen where supply chains co-operate together to advertise. A good example of this is where a holiday destination may advertise the destination with the support of an airline, both sharing the cost of the advertising. Another form of advertising is *recruitment advertising*, which is used to attract new employees and to help to retain those already employed in the organisation. For example, the UK's National Health Service (NHS) launched an extensive nursing recruitment campaign in 2018. The campaign, "We Are the NHS" used television and cinema to drive recruitment of nurses to the NHS and encourage existing nurses to remain in the profession (The Drum, 2018).

Public service announcements (PSAs) are a type of advertising that are aimed at changing the way consumers behave and encouraging citizens to adopt healthy or safe behaviours. The Covid-19 pandemic has provided a range of examples from governments around the globe encouraging their citizens to adopt better hygiene behaviours, socially distance and at times to stay at home to avoid spreading the virus.

 **Stay home**

The UK government ran an emotive public service announcement (PSA) campaign during the second wave of the Covid-19 pandemic in January 2021 asking citizens to: "Stay Home. Protect the NHS. Save Lives". The simple campaign message urging people to stay at home ran across television, radio, press, digital, out-of-home (OOH) and on social media.

Further reading

Anon (2021). New hard-hitting national TV ad urges the nation to stay at home. *GOV.UK*. Retrieved from www.gov.uk/government/news/new-hard-hitting-national-tv-ad-urges-the-nation-to-stay-at-home

Political advertising is used by political parties and lobbying groups to influence political opinion. Political advertising can be used to gain votes at an election or to bring about new legislation. For example, Amnesty International used advertising to lobby the UK government to change legislation on human rights. The organisation ran a double-page advert in *The Times* to ask the government to keep the Human Rights Act. The ad was crowdfunded by supporters and is therefore arguably also an example of *consumer-generated advertising*, which is advertising that has been created by consumers.

 **"Fearless Girl"**

The "Fearless Girl" campaign was created by State Street Global Advisors to champion the promotion of women to senior leadership positions. This award-winning campaign drove awareness that women in corporate leadership positions are good for business and society. As Stephen Tisdale, the Chief Marketing Officer of State Street Global Advisors (2019, p. 25) argues, "Fearless Girl taught us all about the power of diversity. But, as marketer, she taught me something else: that with an authentic message and experience you can do so much more than promote a product. You can start a conversation. You can inspire people to action. And maybe you can even change the world".

Further reading

Tisdale, S. (2019). In Fill, C., & Turnbull, S. (2019). *Marketing Communications: touchpoints, sharing and disruption*. Harlow: Pearson.

Brand activism advertising is advertising created by a brand and supports a particular cause to address a particular environmental or social issue. This is a nascent from of advertising and recognises the power of advertising to effect change in society. For example, Iceland ran the film *Rang-tan* (2018) to highlight the environmental impact of harvesting palm oil in the orang-utan's natural habitat. The campaign aimed to raise awareness of the impact of using palm oil and change consumer behaviour (Ibrahim, 2018).

Brand purpose advertising is used to position the brand with a higher purpose. This may be an ethical, moral or social purpose. For example, in 2004 Dove launched the "Campaign for Real Beauty" which aligned the brand with progressive portrayals of women in advertising. The advertising, which featured realistic portrayals of women, has aligned the brand with a higher purpose.

 **Channel 4 paralympics**

Fill and Turnbull (2019) highlight the case of Channel 4, who created a campaign to drive positive perceptions of disability in the United Kingdom to support the Rio 2016 Paralympic Games. They discuss how, "Channel 4 wanted the campaign to be a positive, life-affirming celebration of the ability of disabled people. The channel developed an integrated strategy with inclusivity at the heart of the campaign" (Fill and Turnbull, 2019, p. 58). The authors provide an overview of the campaign's use of AI and audio-enabled posters to make the campaign more accessible.

Further reading

Fill, C., & Turnbull, S. (2019). *Marketing Communications: touchpoints, sharing and disruption.* Harlow: Pearson.

Femvertising is a form of advertising that portrays women in advertising in more progressive ways and challenges, "gender norms by building stereotype-busting, pro-female messages and images into ads that target women and girls" (#Femverstising Awards, 2021). Examples of femvertising include Microsoft's "We All Win" campaign, which drives female empowerment and inclusion.

Advertising within society

Advertising can influence societal values, beliefs and norms. While advertising has largely been associated with its impact on business, it is hard to ignore the role that advertising has played in changing society over the decades. Advertising has the ability to change behaviours and have a positive impact on society. Middleton and Turnbull (2021) for example highlight the role advertising has played in changing attitudes towards the use of female stereotypes and identify the role that advertisers and agencies have had in changing the portrayal of women in advertising. Their study explores "how advertising got woke" and examines the influence that advertising can have in changing attitudes in society.

Advertising can also change behaviours. In 1985, Levi's relaunched their 501 jeans to target younger audiences and in an attempt to position the brand as cool, created a TV ad which featured Nick Kamen in a 1950's launderette stripping down to his underwear to the track "I Heard It Through the Grapevine" (Fill and Turnbull, 2016). While the advertising had a significant impact on the brand's fortune, increasing Levi's 501 sales by 800%, it also caused a complete change in men's underwear habits. It is reported that the actor was due to wear Y-front underwear in the film but this was not allowed by the censors and so Levi's had him wear boxer shorts instead. As well as making Levi's 501s cool, the advertising also made boxer shorts cool, and as a result led to a dramatic rise in the wearing of boxer shorts (Fill and Turnbull, 2016). Although the objective of the advertising was not to cause a revolution in the male underwear market, it did transform consumer behaviour and change male underwear culture.

Recognition of the power of advertising to change culture within societies has led to the emergence of *brand purpose* advertising campaigns. These campaigns are driven by clear objectives to address challenging issues within societies and bring about cultural change, both in terms of attitudes and behaviour. An example of a brand purpose campaign is Ariel's "#ShareTheLoad" campaign which ran in India to address the issue of gender inequality in Indian households. The campaign used branded content and celebrity endorsements to drive a conversation around the responsibility for household chores. The advertising sparked a national debate around gendered practices in the home and resulted in 3.7 million men in India signing a pledge to #ShareTheLoad with household chores (Fill and Turnbull, 2016).

Advertising   **Support for vulnerable consumers**

Advertising has also been seen to support vulnerable consumer groups. Fletcher-Brown et al. (2020), for example, studied the effect of online advertising on vulnerable consumers and identified that brand advertising can play an important role in supporting vulnerable consumers and addressing societal issues such as stigma associated with women's hair loss due to cancer treatment. They highlight how advertising can be used to provide support to vulnerable groups in developing economies where there is less access to public health services.

Further reading

Fletcher-Brown, J., Turnbull, S., Viglia, G., Chen, T., & Pereira, V. (2020). Vulnerable consumer engagement: How corporate social media can facilitate the replenishment of depleted resources. *International Journal of Research in Marketing, 38*(2), 518–552.

Advertising and the economy

Advertising plays an important role in any nation's economy. The UK advertising sector in particular which provides advertising services to organisations around the world makes a significant contribution to the national economy. The Advertising Association reports that the Office For National Statistics' (ONS) Pink Book 2021 attributes £11 billion to advertising, market research and opinion poll services for the year 2019 (Advertising Association, 2021). The economic data highlights that in 2019, advertising and market research services represented the third largest exporter of services in the United Kingdom after insurance and pension services (£20 billion) and computer services (£12 billion) (Advertising Association, 2021). The top importer of UK advertising services being the United States, followed by France, Germany, Switzerland and Ireland (Advertising Association, 2021).

It is not unusual for global brands to use the services of overseas advertising agencies. Howe-Walsh et al. (2019), for example, investigated advertising agency services in the United Arab Emirates and identified the extent to which creativity is internationally outsourced. The Advertising Association provide a range of examples of brands that use UK advertising agencies to deliver advertising services. For example, Dole, the largest producer of fresh fruit and vegetables, appointed UK advertising agency St Luke's to develop a global campaign to address food insecurity. The campaign, which was created in the United Kingdom featuring Christmas teddy bears, ran across five international markets, including the United States, Japan and New Zealand (Advertising Association, 2021). This example highlights how advertising created in the United Kingdom can be exported and used in other markets and make a contribution to the UK economy.

References

Advertising Association. (2021). *UK advertising exports report 2021*. Retrieved from file:///C:/Users/Sarah/Downloads/UK-Advertising-Exports-Report-2021%20(1).pdf

Anon. (2021). New hard-hitting national TV ad urges the nation to stay at home. *GOV.UK*. Retrieved from www.gov.uk/government/news/new-hard-hitting-national-tv-ad-urges-the-nation-to-stay-at-home

Bullmore, J. (2021). What is advertising? *The Advertising Association*. Retrieved from https://adassoc.org.uk/credos/what-is-advertising/

The Drum. (2018). *NHS: We are the NHS by Mullen Lowe London*. Retrieved from www.thedrum.com/creative-works/project/mullenlowe-london-nhs-we-are-the-nhs

#Femvertising Awards. (2021). *About the #Femvertising awards*. Retrieved from www.femvertisingawards.com/

Fill, C., & Turnbull, S. (2016). *Marketing Communications: discovery, creation and conversations*. Pearson: Harlow.

Fill, C., & Turnbull, S. (2019). *Marketing Communications: touchpoints, sharing and disruption*. Pearson: Harlow.

Fletcher-Brown, J., Turnbull, S., Viglia, G., Chen, T., & Pereira, V. (2020). Vulnerable consumer engagement: How corporate social media can facilitate the replenishment of depleted resources. *International Journal of Research in Marketing*, *38*(2), 518–552.

The History of Advertising Trust. (2013). *Chronology*. Retrieved from www.hatads.org.uk/

Howe-Walsh, L., Turnbull, S., & Budhwar, P. (2019). An investigation into on-sourcing of advertising creativity in an emerging economy: The case of the United Arab Emirates. *Journal of Business Research*, *103*, 356–364.

Ibrahim, M. (2018, November). Iceland's "Rang-tan" ad hits 30m online views and prompts petition. *Campaign*. Retrieved from www.campaignlive.co.uk/article/icelands-rang-tan-ad-hits-30m-online-views-prompts-petition/1498682

Middleton, K., & Turnbull, S. (2021). How advertising got "woke". The institutional role of advertising in the emergence of gender progressive market logics and practices. *Marketing Theory* [In press].

Richards, J. I., & Curran, C. M. (2002). Oracles on "advertising": Searching for a definition. *Journal of Advertising*, *31*(2), 63–77.

Tisdale, S. (2019). In Fill, C. & Turnbull, S. (2019). *Marketing Communications: touchpoints, sharing and disruption*. Pearson: Harlow.

Tomkovick, C., Yelkur, R., & Christians, L. (2001). The USA's biggest marketing event keeps getting bigger: An in-depth look at Super Bowl advertising in the 1990s. *Journal of Marketing Communications*, *7*(2), 89–108.

Turnbull, S. (2019). Lessons from the United Kingdom: Employability, brand responsibility, and a nation of "ad lovers". *Journal of Advertising Education*, *23*(2), 140–141.

Wieden + Kennedy. (2010). *P&G: Thank you, mom*. Retrieved from www.wk.com/work/p-and-g-thank-you-mom/

2 Advertising
Planning and strategy

Learning outcomes

This chapter aims to enable readers to:

1 Explain how advertising campaigns are planned
2 Consider how budgets and objectives are set
3 Examine the role of targeting, insight and the consumer decision journey
4 Understand the role of measurement
5 Consider further reading on planning and strategy issues

Campaign planning

There are a number of important elements that need to be considered by advertisers and their agencies when developing communications strategy. It is important to begin by considering the current position of the brand within the market and to examine where the brand is positioned in the context of its competitors. Having evaluated the current situation, the brand then needs to consider where it wants to be positioned. This leads to setting clear objectives and a determination of the budget allocation that will support the strategy.

When developing a strategy, advertisers need to consider who they intend to target and the consumer journey. They will need to gain insights about the target audience and understand what messages will resonate with them and which channels will be the best to reach them. It is also important to ensure that the strategy can be evaluated as it is deployed to allow for optimisation and measurement.

DOI: 10.4324/9781003175551-2

Positioning

Brands can evaluate their current position using frameworks such as PESTLE or SWOT. The PESTLE framework allows brands to consider the wider environmental forces that may influence strategy decisions:

- Political: Governmental and regulatory influences.
- Economic: Economic factors such as tax.
- Social: Societal influences, including culture.
- Technological: New technologies and digital developments.
- Legal: Legislation.
- Environment: Sustainability and environmental influences.

The strength and weakness of the brand need to be evaluated alongside the potential opportunities and threats that are known:

- Strengths: What strengths does the brand have in the market? What is the current market share positioning of the brand versus the competitors? What are the distribution strengths of the brand?
- Weaknesses: Where are the current weaknesses of the brand? How does the price compare to competitors pricing? How do consumers perceive the quality of the brand?
- Opportunities: Is there scope to increase pricing? Is there an opportunity to increase distribution? What opportunities exist to change perceptions and attitudes about the brand? Is there an opportunity to increase share of voice?
- Threats: What is the threat from the competitor brands? What is the share of market of competitive brands?

Having evaluated the current position of the brand and identified the opportunities that may exist, a positioning can be determined. Positioning allows a brand to stand out in a cluttered media environment and distinguishes the brand from others in the market. It also provides a frame of reference for the consumer and allows associations which will help the consumer connect with the brand. Young (2017) argues that there are five main positions that brands can assume in the market: market leader, follower, premium, least cost, niche. These are defined as:

- Market leader: These brands dominate with the largest share of market. Tesco for example would be seen as a market leader among supermarket brands. Similarly, British Airways could be seen as the UK market leader in the airline category.

- Follower: The follower does not have as large a share of market as the market leader, but may challenge the leader in the future (Young, 2017). An example of a follower may be Asda in the supermarket sector.
- Premium: These brands are premium priced and appeal to consumers who often have higher disposable incomes. Although luxury brands such as Louis Vuitton and Chanel may be included in this category, other premium brands can be seen in food categories (e.g., Fortnum and Mason).
- Least cost: These brands provide a low-price offering. Examples include Lidl, Aldi and Ryan Air.
- Niche: Niche brands position themselves as providing a sufficiently different offering to other brands in the same category. The difference may be from a range of elements such as price, distribution, product or place of manufacture. Graze snacks are a good example of a niche brand.

In addition to Young's typology of brand positions, it is arguable that two other categories exist. They are purpose brands and luxury brands. These are defined as:

- Purpose brands: These brands are positioned as brands that support societal issues such as poverty, inequality or sustainability. An example of this type of brand is Toms, who pledge to give a pair of shoes to a child in need for every pair of shoes purchased.
- Luxury: Luxury brands are those that are perceived to be higher in price, quality, aesthetics or other values. Luxury brands have been defined as, "high quality, expensive and non-essential products and services that appear to be rare, exclusive, prestigious, and authentic and offer high levels of symbolic and emotional/hedonic values through customer experiences" (Tynan et al., 2010, p. 1158). Examples of luxury brands include Versace.

Setting objectives

Setting clear objectives is one of the most important elements of planning a campaign. Having clearly defined goals provides direction for all members of the communications team and helps to keep the campaign focussed while it is in progress. It also provides an opportunity to evaluate and measure outcomes against pre-defined goals.

 **Baileys: Setting communications, marketing and business objectives**

Baileys's "Don't Mind If I Baileys" campaign set a clear mix of objectives for communications, marketing and business to provide direction for all members of the planning team. Carrington et al. (2020, p. 1) outline the objectives set by the brand:

1   Communications objective: "Create enjoyable communications that renew the product's intrinsically delicious appeal".
2   Marketing objective: "Increase the perceived versatility of the Baileys liquid, as efficiently as possible".
3   Commercial objective: "Reverse volume sales decline in our key global markets and restore internal belief in the brand".

Each objective was accompanied by a specific Key Performance Indicator (KPI) which allowed the effectiveness of the campaign to be monitored, measured and evaluated.

Further reading

Carrington, J., McGuinness, N., Wijegoonewardene, V., Cunningham, S., Deykin, A., Holgate, V., da Fonseca, C., McGhee, R., Linford, M. Price, P., Mackay-Sinclair, K. (2020). Baileys: From forgotten icon to global treat. *Institute of Practitioners in Advertising*, Silver, IPA Effectiveness Awards. Retrieved from www.warc.com/content/article/baileys-from-forgotten-icon-to-global-treat/133195

It is important to set objectives at the planning stage of a campaign so that they can be agreed between the advertiser and agency and to enable evaluation later on. Objectives should be precise and clearly articulated in the brief.

While setting objectives that are seen to be SMART – specific, measurable, achievable, relevant and time-bound – has been a framework commonly used across communications for decades, it is suggested that contemporary advertising should also consider that communications plans be equality-driven and responsible.

 **Setting "SMARTER" objectives**

To ensure campaign objectives are clear each one should be SMARTER:

- Specific: Clear and unambiguous statement of desired outcome.
- Measurable: A quantitative or qualitative outcome.
- Achievable: Attainable with the time and resources of the campaign.
- Relevant: Aligned to the business strategy.
- Time-bound: Provide a clear timeframe for results to be achieved.
- Equality-driven: Ensure that no individuals or groups are disadvantaged and considers inclusivity and diversity.
- Responsible: Consider the moral and ethical implications of the campaign.

The "SMARTER" form of objective setting ensures that the campaign takes inclusivity and diversity into account to avoid disadvantaging any individuals or groups. As well as being equality driven, campaigns should also be responsible and ensure that consideration is given to the moral and ethical dimensions of the campaign.

Further reading

Fill, C., & Turnbull, S. (2019). *Marketing Communications: touchpoints, sharing and disruption*. Harlow: Pearson.

Setting budgets

How much to spend on advertising is an important consideration in planning. There are numerous ways that have been used for setting budgets and many brands typically use some form of benchmark to determine the advertising budget. Haigh (2020) provides a review of how to set marketing budgets and identifies a number of common benchmarks used to set budgets:

- Industry benchmarks (% sales): This takes into account the spend by other brands in the same category.

- Share of voice: Represents the relative share of media spend in comparison to competitors in the same category. There is seen to be a strong relationship between share of voice (SOV) and share of market (SOM) such that if a brand wishes to increase their SOM, they should plan to spend more and increase their SOV (for a full review of this relationship see Jones, 1990).
- Industry marketing split: Benchmarking against the split made between media channels.
- Customer expectation benchmarks: Based on channel selection to reach target audience.
- Company historic benchmarks: Based on previous year's spend.
- Objectives/tasks benchmarks: Calculated to achieve what the task requires.

Targeting, insight and the consumer decision journey

Advertising strategy needs to be targeted and this means that planners need to determine who they wish to target with their messaging. It also requires an understanding of consumers to help ensure that messages resonate with target audiences. Zohrer (2017) suggest that brands need to understand a number of factors when evaluating a target audience:

- Who is the target audience: What are their socio-demographics/ psychographics?
- What are their habits: What channels do they watch? How do they consume media?
- When are they watching: What hours in the day are audiences watching? What times of the year are they consuming content? What impact do factors such as weather have on consumption?

Insight is seen as a valuable resource when planning campaigns. Knowles (2020, p. 1) cites the Head of Planning at agency Lowe & Partners as defining insight as, "a glimpse inside the mind of the target audience, shining a light on a possible solution to the problem we have defined. Insight increases the chances of creative breakthrough, makes the creative process less random, and incites behaviour change". Such insight allows creatives to develop campaigns which engage with audiences.

Advertising Brief **Using insight – Persil**

Insight provides "a profound and useful understanding of a person, a thing, a situation, or an issue" Knowles (2020, p. 1). The author argues that insight encourages questioning about established conceptualisations of people and objects, allowing new ways of thinking to emerge. Knowles (2020, p. 1) outlines the insight underpinning the Persil "Dirt is Good" campaign as part of a three-stage process, "Since the 1920s, laundry ads told mums off if their kids' clothes weren't whiter than white" [stage 1], because of "The misperception that parenthood is more about protection from unseen evils than it is about development" [stage 2], which means "A generation of children rarely go outside and don't grow through experimentation" [stage 3]. This fresh insight led to the creation of the "Dirt is Good" campaign, which encouraged parents to allow their children to go outside and not be afraid of getting clothes dirty.

Further reading

Knowles, S. (2020, October). How to be insightful. *WARC Best Practice.* Retrieved from www.warc.com/content/article/bestprac/how-to-be-insightful/134594

A good understanding of the target audience and consumer insight will allow brands to map out the consumer decision journey. This enables a brand to understand all the potential touchpoints where they engage with audiences. In contrast to previous conceptualisations of the consumer journey which have depicted the purchase journey operating as a funnel, Court et al. (2009) provide a consumer decision journey which is circular. This outlines the decision-making process as having four main stages: Initial consideration, active evaluation, closure and postpurchase, with each phase operating within a circular framework. The authors highlight the significance of each phase in the journey and suggest that in the first stage of initial consideration, consumers consider an initial set of brands based on both consumer's perceptions and their exposure to touchpoints. They suggest that a trigger can occur at this stage to influence perceptions. The second phase of active evaluation represents the stage when consumers undertake research about possible purchases and add or remove brands from their consideration. The third phase, closure, is when the consumer buys the brand, and the fourth phase, postpurchase, is the stage when the consumer experiences the brand. The authors highlight that the postpurchase phase will inform the next decision journey (Court et al., 2009). This conceptualisation of the consumer decision journey by Court et al. (2009) is used by practitioners for planning communications and identifying the touchpoints that can help at each phase of the journey. The consumer decision journey is also referred to in Chapter 3 and has been extended to provide a new theory of advertising. The trigger theory of advertising offers a novel framework to help us better understand how advertising works.

Such decision journey mapping is commonplace in agencies which use the maps to identify touchpoints and gain a holistic view of the consumer journey. Siantonas (2017, p. 1) explains how to map out a consumer journey for a brand and argues that this mapping allows brands to build an ecosystem to represent, "all the possible touchpoints that a customer can come into contact with on their journey. Each touchpoint is linked to others in a specific way, depending on where a customer can go once they've interacted with a touchpoint". He suggests that consumer journeys should be part of a much wider organisational ecosystem to ensure that communications reach the target audience at the right time and in the right place.

Measurement

Measurement is an important aspect of campaign planning and should be considered at the early stages of planning and included in any brief. Setting SMARTER objectives with specific goals to be achieved in the campaign is one way to help with measurement. Chapter 9 discusses the measurement techniques and metrics used to evaluate campaigns. The chapter highlights the different stages of an advertising campaign that advertisers may wish to evaluate, and outlines how creative ideas can be tested during the creative development stage. The chapter also highlights how campaigns should be monitored to ensure they optimise performance and evaluated on their completion to determine whether the campaign has met the objectives set.

References

Carrington, J., McGuinness, N., Wijegoonewardene, V., Cunningham, S., Deykin, A., Holgate, V., da Fonseca, C., McGhee, R., Linford, M., Price, P., & Mackay-Sinclair, K. (2020). Baileys: From forgotten icon to global treat. *Institute of Practitioners in Advertising*, Silver, IPA Effectiveness Awards. Retrieved from www.warc.com/content/article/baileys-from-forgotten-icon-to-global-treat/133195

Court, D., Elzinger, D., Mulder, S., & Jørgen Vetvik, O. (2009, June 1). The consumer decision journey (2009). *McKinsey Quarterly*. Retrieved from www.mckinsey.com/business-functions/marketing-and-sales/our-insights/the-consumer-decision-journey

Fill, C., & Turnbull, S. (2019). *Marketing Communications: touchpoints, sharing and disruption*. Pearson: Harlow.

Haigh, A. (2020). How to set marketing budgets. *Brand Finance White Paper*, *WARC*. Retrieved from www.warc.com/content/article/warc-exclusive/how-to-set-marketing-budgets/134803

Jones, J. P. (1990). Ad spending: Maintaining market share. *Harvard Business Review*, *68*(1), 38–42.

Knowles, S. (2020, October). How to be insightful. *WARC Best Practice*. Retrieved from www.warc.com/content/article/bestprac/how-to-be-insightful/134594

Siantonas, N. (2017, August). How to map the consumer journey. *WARC Best Practice*, p. 1. Retrieved from www.warc.com/content/article/bestprac/how-to-map-the-customer-journey/112128

Tynan, C., McKechnie, S., & Chhuon, C. (2010). Co-creating value for luxury brands. *Journal of Business Research*, *63*(11), 1156–1163.

Young, L. (2017, February). How to use brand positioning effectively. *WARC Best Practice*. Retrieved from www.warc.com/content/article/bestprac/how-to-use-brand-positioning-effectively/94829#:~:text=How%20to%20use,Practice%2C%20February%202017

Zohrer, R. (2017, December). 3 critical steps in defining and reaching an audience through advertising. *Admap Magazine*. Retrieved from www.warc.com/content/article/3_critical_steps_in_defining_and_reaching_an_audience_through_advertising/117256

3 Advertising theory

Learning outcomes

This chapter aims to enable readers to:

1   Understand how advertising works
2   Explain the different models of advertising
3   Examine how practitioners think advertising works
4   Evaluate the trigger theory of advertising
5   Consider further reading on advertising theory

How advertising works

There have been a number of models over the last century which offer an explanation of how advertising works. The first advertising model was the attention, interest, desire, and action model (AIDA) proposed by Elias St. Elmo Lewis in 1898. While Lewis's model is over 100 years old, it is still covered in most professional and academic advertising courses today. This may in part be due to its simplicity, but also because it has not been discounted as an explanation of how advertising works.

The AIDA model suggests that audiences move through four sequential stages, starting with *attention*. In today's media environment the notion that advertising needs to capture audience attention seems more important than ever. The second stage is *interest* and signifies a state where audiences are interested in the message and/or brand. The next stage is *desire*, which refers to the audience's moving to a step of wanting the product/service. The last stage is *action*. As the model was initially developed as a sales model, this final stage originally represented a sale being made. Strong (1925) applied Lewis's model to advertising and suggests that the AIDA model should be seen in terms of,

DOI: 10.4324/9781003175551-3

"four states of consciousness which must pass through the mind of the prospect before he will buy. In other words, if the prospect experiences attention, interest, desire, he will be more likely to act; and consequently an advertisement or sales talk must be planned to arouse these states in him".

(Strong, 1925, p. 76)

Advertising Brief **AIDA model**

The AIDA model provides an explanation of how advertising works and suggests a four stage process whereby audiences move from initial attention through to an action, providing an identifiable outcome (Lewis 1898 cited in Strong, 1925):

- Stage one: Attention
- Stage two: Interest
- Stage three: Desire
- Stage four: Action

Some authors have been critical of such sequential models and argue that attention is not always required for an ad to be effective (Heath and Feldwick, 2008). It is also important to consider what levels of attention may be required and what is considered as a sufficient level of attention. Furthermore, the model assumes that if audiences pay attention to advertising and find it interesting, they will progress to stage three, desire, and finally stage four, action. However, there are many ads that consumers pay attention to and find interesting that do not lead to desire and action.

Further reading

Heath, R., & Feldwick, P. (2008). Fifty years using the wrong model of advertising. *International Journal of Market Research*, *50*(1), 29–59.

The notion that advertising works to "funnel" sales is reflected in many of the advertising models which have followed on from Lewis's AIDA model. Vakratsas and Ambler (1999, p. 27) provide a comprehensive review of the sequential models and identify seven main taxonomies of models of how advertising works and suggest that each is associated with a clear sequence of effects as follow:

- Market response: With no advertising effects considered
- Cognitive information: Leading to a "think" effect
- Pure affect: Leading to a "feel" effect
- Persuasive hierarchy: With an effect of "think-feel-do"
- Low-involvement hierarchy: With an effect of "think-do-feel"
- Integrative: No fixed sequence of effects
- Hierarchy-free: No hierarchy

The persuasive hierarchy models which suggest a fixed order in which the effects occur have made a significant contribution to our understanding of how advertising works and been widely used in advertising research (Vakratsas and Ambler, 1999). One of the persuasive hierarchy models which is highlighted by Vakratas and Ambler is the model presented by Lavidge and Steiner (1961). This model suggests that advertising works through a hierarchy of six discreet stages (Lavidge and Steiner, 1961).

 **Hierarchy-of-effects model**

Lavidge and Steiner (1961, p. 61) offer a six-step hierarchy-of-effects model as follows:

- Step one: Awareness
- Step two: Knowledge
- Step three: Liking
- Step four: Preference
- Step five: Conviction
- Step six: Purchase

Lavidge and Steiner (1961, p. 59) argue, "consumers normally do not switch from disinterested individuals to convinced purchasers in one instantaneous step. Rather, they approach the ultimate purchase through a process or series of steps in which the actual purchase is but the final threshold". The model proposed by the authors suggests a funnel effect and the ultimate goal of the process being a purchase.

Further reading

Lavidge, R. J., & Steiner, G. A. (1961). A model for predictive measurements of advertising effectiveness. *Journal of Marketing, 25*(6), 59–62.

An alternative approach for understanding how advertising works is the elaboration likelihood model (ELM) proposed by Petty and Cacioppo (1984). The ELM offers an alternative framework to explain how advertising works and is recognised as one of the most influential and valuable models in marketing communications (Kitchen et al., 2014). Widely used in advertising research, the ELM offers a simple framework that explains how persuasion occurs.

The term "elaboration likelihood" refers to, "the likelihood one [consumer] engages in issue-relevant thinking with the aim of determining the merits of the argument for a position" (Petty and Cacioppo, 1984, p. 3). The ELM conceptualises two routes to persuasion in advertising: the central route and the peripheral routes. Petty and Cacioppo (1984) argue that the two routes to persuasion are determined by consumers' motivation and ability to engage in elaboration or, "issue-relevant thinking" (p. 2). Depending on whether a consumer is motivated or not to engage in such thinking, determines whether the route is "central" or "peripheral".

Despite being a popular model, the ELM has been criticised for its relevance to the digital landscape (Kitchen et al., 2014). Such criticism is not surprising when you consider the model was developed to explain persuasion in the 1980s before digital channels were created.

Advertising Brief **The elaboration likelihood model**

The elaboration likelihood model (Petty and Cacioppo, 1984) suggests advertising works in two ways depending on the motivation and ability to think about the argument presented in the advertising. When consumers are motivated and engaged, elaboration is seen to be high, meaning:

- Attention will be given to the advertising.
- Consumers will draw on past experiences and imagery that are relevant to the advertising and elaborate on the message using these associations.
- Consumers will evaluate the message.

Petty and Cacioppo (1984) suggest that where elaboration is high, the central route is taken and cognitive resources should be available to support consumers who are more likely to act upon their attitudes. In contrast, where elaboration likelihood is low, consumers will conserve their cognitive resources and avoid involvement in the advertising. They may choose instead to skip the advertising or be distracted by another task. In this case, where no intrinsic link exists to the message or stimulus, Petty and Cacioppo (1984) suggest a peripheral route, using peripheral cues is more likely.

Further reading

Cacioppo, J. T., & Petty, R. E. (1984). The elaboration likelihood model of persuasion. *ACR North American Advances.*
Kitchen, P. J., Kerr, G., Schultz, D. E., McColl, R., & Pals, H. (2014). The elaboration likelihood model: Review, critique and research agenda. *European Journal of Marketing, 48*(11/12), 2033–2050.

How practitioners think advertising works

There has always been a gap between academic views of how advertising works and the views of those working in the industry. While there are differences between academics and practitioners, there are many common notions about how advertising works. One area that most academic and practitioners would agree upon is that advertising does work.

Nyilasy and Reid (2009) undertook a study to examine how agency practitioners think advertising works. They interviewed senior advertising agency creatives, planners and account directors to elicit "quasi- theoretical" views about advertising. Their findings identified two main theoretical notions about how advertising works: "break through and engage" and "mutation of effects".

The model of "break through and engage" was seen as a simple two-step process whereby the advertising created awareness (step one) and then engaged audiences (step two). The two-stage sequence was seen as important because in order to engage audiences, the practitioners saw the need to draw attention to the advertising first. The practitioners emphasised the importance of creating a level of brand awareness first before any impact on attitude or behaviour could be achieved (Nyilasy and Reid, 2009).

In the second model identified by Nyilasy and Reid (2009, p. 87), "mutation of effects", the advertising practitioners saw consumers as, "a somewhat antagonistic group, who actively resist ad influence attempts. At the heart of this resistance is knowledge about what advertisers are planning on doing". This very simple sequential model does not include any further stages to suggest the engagement will lead to any action such as trial.

A new framework to conceptualise how advertising works: Advertising trigger theory (ATT)

Many of the advertising models which have been outlined in this chapter are over 50 years old and although they may still be used to help explain how advertising works, there is concern that some may not be reflective of the modern advertising landscape. Earlier models of advertising are largely based on a "sales funnel" using a sequence of steps which lead to a purchase. However, advertising has evolved to have a wider role in society and the objectives of an advertising campaign are not always intended to result in the sale of a product or service. For example, Fletcher-Brown et al. (2021) identified that an Indian hair brand used social media to provide resources to vulnerable consumers. Their study highlighted how media platforms are being employed to raise awareness of societal issues and improve the lives of cancer sufferers. Other campaigns have been used to support a positioning of brand purpose and to address social, economic or environmental issues.

In addition to the changing role of advertising in society, the emergence of digital media and the increasingly cluttered media landscape means that brands need to work much harder to breakthrough in order to reach consumers. To gain the attention of the audience, advertisers use disruptive techniques such as creative messaging or creative use of media. For example, Burger King's "Google Home of the Whopper" campaign disrupted Google home devices to gain attention. The brand created a 15-second TV ad to activate Google home devices and interact with the advertising message (Google Home of the Whopper Burger, 2017). The campaign enabled the brand to deliver messages about ingredients in the Whopper through consumers' home devices. The Google Home of the Whopper is just one of many examples where creative media use has enabled a brand to interrupt consumers activity. New media platforms and mobile technology have provided increased opportunities for advertisers to gain consumers' attention in new contexts. Media such as "digital out-of-home" (DOOH) and mobile technology has meant that advertisers can be reached and interrupted by advertising in a greater variety of locations and in a wider range of contexts. For example, consumers can be targeted using geolocation as they approach a retail outlet or while they are in a supermarket shopping.

Having "disrupted" or captured the attention of the consumer, advertisers need to engage audiences. This may be achieved through rational or emotional appeals. Emotional appeals have become increasingly used by advertisers to engage audiences. For example, John Lewis's Christmas advertising has used storytelling and an emotional route to engage audiences. However, well executed rational appeals can be equally engaging. In many cases, advertisers will choose to combine rational and emotional elements to ensure rational product benefits are communicated in an emotive manner. For example, Audi chose to use humour in their campaign "Clowns", which featured clowns causing havoc on the road and at the same time allowed the brand to demonstrate the high-tech safety features of their cars, including adaptive cruise control and park assist (Kiefer, 2017).

There are many techniques and devices used by advertisers to engage audiences in advertising. Some advertisers choose to use celebrities to front their advertising in order to engage audiences. Others have used storytelling, product demonstration, surrealism or found novel approaches to entertain audiences. The iconic Cadbury's gorilla ad, for example, featured a gorilla playing drums to the Phil Collins track "In the Air Tonight". There was no overt product message, and apart from the purple background in the advertising until the end frame of the film, there were few cues to indicate who the advertiser was. As well as providing novelty, audiences were engaged in the advertising because they wanted to find out who the advertiser was. Crafting creative campaigns to engage audiences is a highly skilled process and most brands choose to engage the specialist services of an advertising agency to achieve this.

Advertising Brief   Advertising trigger theory (ATT)

The trigger theory of advertising provides an alternative explanation of how advertising works. This theory builds on the conceptualisation of Court et al. (2009) discussed in Chapter 2 that the consumer decision journey should not be seen as a funnel, but rather a series of circular phases and influenced by touchpoints and a trigger to influence the initial consideration of a brand. The trigger theory of advertising extends the conceptualisation of the consumer decision journey to offer a new theory of advertising, providing a novel framework to help us better understand how advertising works.

The model conceptualises the process of advertising as a three-stage process: Disrupt, engage and trigger (see Figure 3.1). The first stage, "Disrupt", gains the attention of the audience. The second stage, "engage", connects with the audience, and the third stage, "trigger", is the encouragement to change behaviour or attitude. While this final stage may be the encouragement to try a new product or service, it equally represents the attitudinal or behavioural change such as the UK government's "Stay Home" campaign described in Chapter 1.

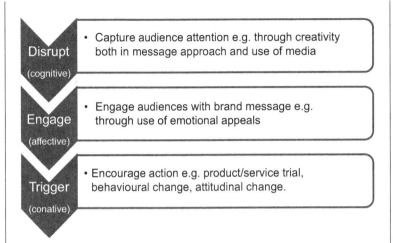

Figure 3.1 Trigger theory: Stages explaining how advertising works

While the trigger theory stages are linear, it is the conceptualisation of these stages applied across the consumer journey that offers a fresh understanding of how advertising works in practice. Advertising should be seen as part of the consumer journey and advertisers need to understand the role that each channel has within that journey. Thus, the trigger theory offers a more holistic understanding of advertising as a process within the overall consumer journey. To be effective, advertising needs to be planned to reach and engage consumers at the right time of the day and through the right channel. Figure 3.2 illustrates how the triggers might be planned by an advertiser to engage audiences along the consumer journey. A variety of channels may be used at different times throughout the day according to the context of the product and message. For example, a restaurant chain may use a local radio channel to deliver the message while audiences are driving to work in the morning, an out-of-home (OOH) billboard may be used to engage audiences while they walk to the shops to buy lunch during the day and a cinema ad may be used in the evening as a final trigger to encourage trying dinner at the restaurant nearby the cinema.

Conceptualising how advertising works within the context of the customer journey sees advertising as an ongoing process. Triggers are delivered across the consumer journey and continue being delivered even after an action or behavioural change has taken place. The ATT

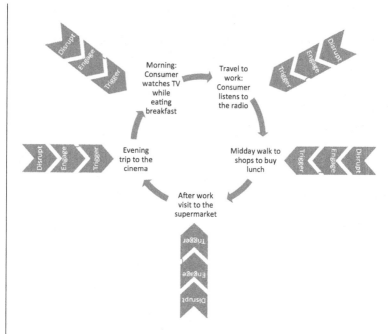

Figure 3.2 Reaching audiences along the consumer journey

theory is offered for future discussion and examination as a more contemporary conceptualisation of how advertising works.

References

Cacioppo, J. T., & Petty, R. E. (1984). The elaboration likelihood model of persuasion. *ACR North American Advances.*

Court, D., Elzinger, D., Mulder, S., & Jørgen Vetvik, O. (2009, June 1). The consumer decision journey (2009). *McKinsey Quarterly.* Retrieved from www.mckinsey.com/business-functions/marketing-and-sales/our-insights/the-consumer-decision-journey

Fletcher-Brown, J., Turnbull, S., Viglia, G., Chen, T., & Pereira, V. (2021). Vulnerable consumer engagement: How corporate social media can facilitate the replenishment of depleted resources. *International Journal of Research in Marketing, 38*(2), 518–529.

Google Home of the Whopper Burger. (2017). Retrieved from YouTube www.youtube.com/watch?v=OUj8SUoJ-ZM

Heath, R., & Feldwick, P. (2008). Fifty years using the wrong model of advertising. *International Journal of Market Research, 50*(1), 29–59.

Kiefer, B. (2017, September 28). Audi sends in the clowns for big-budget tech campaign. *Campaign.* Retrieved from www.campaignlive.co.uk/article/audi-sends-clowns-big-budget-tech-campaign/1445813

Kitchen, P. J., Kerr, G., Schultz, D. E., McColl, R., & Pals, H. (2014). The elaboration likelihood model: Review, critique and research agenda. *European Journal of Marketing, 48*(11/12), 2033–2050.

Lavidge, R. J., & Steiner, G. A. (1961). A model for predictive measurements of advertising effectiveness. *Journal of Marketing, 25*(6), 59–62.

Nyilasy, G., & Reid, L. N. (2009). Agency practitioner theories of how advertising works. *Journal of Advertising, 38*(3), 81–96.

Petty, R. E., & Cacioppo, J. T. (1984). Source factors and the elaboration likelihood model of persuasion. *ACR North American Advances.*

Strong, E. K., Jr. (1925). Theories of selling. *Journal of Applied Psychology, 9*(1), 75–86.

Vakratsas, D., & Ambler, T. (1999). How advertising works: What do we really know? *Journal of Marketing, 63*(1), 26–43.

4 Advertising appeals

Learning outcomes

This chapter aims to enable readers to:

1 Examine the different types of advertising appeals
2 Evaluate rational appeals used in advertising
3 Understand the use of emotional appeals used in advertising
4 Explain why the use of some appeals is controversial
5 Consider further reading on advertising appeals

Types of appeal

Advertisers usually choose between using rational or emotional appeals. Rational appeals are used more often for products or services where there is extended decision-making involved and where information is needed to help the consumer in their decision. In contrast, emotional appeals are more broadly aligned to those products that do not require considerable thought processing and where the decision is often made quickly.

Rational appeals

Rational appeals can include a variety of approaches including;

- Demonstration
- Price-led
- Comparison
- Science-led

The demonstration of products in advertising is a well-trodden creative path and has become synonymous over the years with products such as batteries, household cleaning products and shampoos. The advantage of this type of appeal is that brands can show how their products can be used and highlight

DOI: 10.4324/9781003175551-4

a product's benefits. A criticism of demonstration appeals in the past has been that many of those in the household cleaning category have relied on women to be the demonstrator and thus the advertising has used gendered stereotypes. However, new gender stereotyping rules introduced by the Advertising Standards Authority (ASA), which came into effect in the United Kingdom in 2018, state that ads, "must not include gender stereotypes that are likely to cause harm, or serious or widespread offence" (ASA, 2019). While this new guidance has not stopped all advertisers creating advertising appeals that suggest cleaning the home is the responsibility of women, it does allow the ASA to investigate complaints and ban offensive advertising.

Advertising Brief   **Avoiding gender stereotyping**

The ASA introduced guiding principles on gender stereotyping in advertising. Their guidance outlines that ads may use people undertaking gender-stereotypical roles such as a woman doing the housework or a man doing do-it-yourself projects. However, their guidance makes clear that advertisers, "should take care to avoid suggesting that stereotypical roles or characteristics are:

- always uniquely associated with one gender;
- the only options available to one gender;
- never carried out or displayed by another gender" (Anon, 2021).

Although the ASA has introduced regulations to remove gender stereotyping from UK advertising, many other countries continue to see stereotypes being used. Middleton et al. (2020) for example identified the prevalent use of gender stereotypes used in Brazilian advertising, highlighting the cultural differences in practice.

Further reading

Anon (2021). *Advertising standards authority.* Advertising guidance on depicting gender stereotypes likely to cause harm or serious or widespread offence. Retrieved from www.asa.org.uk/uploads/assets/6c98e678-8eb7-4f9f-8e5d99491382c665/guidance-on-depicting-gender-stereotypes.pdf

Middleton, K., Thompson-Whiteside, H., Turnbull, S., & Fletcher-Brown, J. (2022). How consumers subvert advertising through rhetorical institutional work. *Psychology & Marketing, 39*(3), 634–646.

Middleton, K., Turnbull, S., & de Oliveira, M. J. (2020). Female role portrayals in Brazilian advertising: Are outdated cultural stereotypes preventing change? *International Journal of Advertising, 39*(5), 679–698.

Price-led appeals are also used to deliver rational messages based on the price advantage of products or services. Many supermarkets have used this advertising route to support in-store price promotions and drive short-term sales. Price-led appeals have also been used by supermarkets to gain market share by comparing product pricing with competitive retailers. For example, the discount grocery retailer Aldi has used price-led appeals in their advertising to contrast the price of their own label products with branded labels. The retailer has shown comparative prices in the advertising appeals to support their claims of price value.

Advertisers have also used appeals with product comparisons. Such comparative advertising has been used by a variety of products and services. For example, the Duracell bunny has been used since 1973 by the brand to compare the life of alkaline batteries to ordinary zinc carbon batteries (Duracell, 2021). The brand's iconic comparative advertising has shown the Duracell bunny winning races against ordinary zinc carbon battery bunnies. There are, however, a number of key considerations that brands need to take into account if they wish to use this style of advertising. The ASA (2021, p. 1) sets out four factors that advertiser need to consider to ensure that they are compliant with advertising regulations and avoid misleading consumers:

- What claim do you want to make?
- Is it a comparison with an identifiable competitor?
- Are you comparing the right things?
- Is the comparison verifiable?

The ASA highlights that advertiser need to consider the claim they are making in their advertising. For example, is the advertiser claiming they are "best-selling", "leading", "no.1", "premier" or "best" and if so, documentary evidence is needed to support the claim. Similarly, evidence to support claims which compare the product or service to identifiable competitors is needed. Furthermore, the ASA highlights the need for advertisers to ensure the basis of the claim is clear, consumers are not misled and the comparison is verifiable (ASA, 2021).

Science-led appeals are an effective means of communicating factual information about the product. Such appeals have been popular with brands across a range of categories. For example, women's face cream brands have over the decades use this route to deliver advertising featuring new vitamins or acids that will improve consumers' skin. Similarly, car brands have included the technological features of their new vehicles. For example, Audi's 'clowns' ad focussed on the car's LED headlights and Audi's park assist feature to help drivers park their car in tight parking spaces. The campaign used the tagline "Audi technology. Clown proof", which reflected the importance of the technology in the positioning (Kiefer, 2017).

Emotional appeals

Just as there are a large range of emotions, there are also a number of different emotional routes that advertisers can use. Some of the more common emotional appeals include:

- Humour
- Fear
- Guilt
- Shock

Humour is a powerful emotion and has been used with great effect to engage audiences. This is an advantage for advertisers who are struggling to break through the clutter and gain the attention of audiences in a fragmented media landscape. Mulcahy (2019, p. 1) argues that,

> "Using humor in marketing is a tried and tested strategy for brands to ensure that their campaign is impactful and remains memorable for audiences. Tapping into what makes consumers laugh can create a more meaningful relationship between a brand and its target audience".

While humour appeals can be highly engaging, care needs to be taken however not to cause offense to audiences. The number of complaints received by the ASA about humorous advertising suggests that advertisers need to be very careful to avoid causing offense to audiences or harming vulnerable consumers.

Advertising Brief **Using comedy to reduce rail deaths**

"Dumb Ways to Die" is an award-winning campaign developed to reduce the number of deaths on Melbourne Metro train services. The public service video featuring animated characters and a catchy theme song made fun of the way that people could die. Characters were shown swimming with piranhas and prodding bears. The dark humour and amusing lyrics struck a comedic note with audiences and the video became an internet sensation shared on YouTube more than 50 million times (Sweney, 2013). The campaign highlights how humorous appeals can engage audiences and the extent to which consumers are willing to share funny content.

Further reading

Dumb Ways to Die website. Retrieved from www.dumbwaystodie.com/
Mulcahy, E. (2019, June 27). Humor marketing: Five ads that got consumers laughing. *The Drum*. Retrieved from www.thedrum.com/news/2019/06/27/humor-marketing-five-ads-got-consumers-laughing
Sweney, M. (2013, June 22). Cannes Lions: Dumb ways to die scoops top award. *The Guardian*. Retrieved from www.theguardian.com/media/2013/jun/22/cannes-lions-advertising-awards

Fear is another powerful emotion that advertisers use in advertising appeals and has been used in the past by a variety of organisations and brands, including public service campaigns. For example, the UK Department of Health used a fear appeal in their 1980's HIV/AIDS campaign, "Don't Die of Ignorance". The film, which was shot in darkness, featured a gravestone being carved and had a menacing voice-over and delivered the health message with frightening effect (Darby, 2020). Darby (2020, p. 1) argues, however, that it is not just public service campaigns for health, anti-smoking or anti-drunk driving that use fear appeals, and suggests that the use of fear within advertising is more widespread: "FMCG categories, including cleaning products and cosmetics, have traditionally based much of their advertising upon generating a low-grade sense of fear among audiences – of lacking the perfect body, the perfect home, the perfect family".

Advertisers should be careful, however, to avoid arousing excessive fear in audiences, especially when targeting vulnerable or elderly consumers (ASA, 2021). The ASA provides an example of a complaint which was upheld against a 2012 advertising campaign which was seen to cause excessive fear for an electrical company which claimed, "Old fuse boards can cause fires and electrical accidents can kill you"(ASA, 2021). In recent years, many advertisers have moved away from using fear appeals as they have found them to be less effective at changing consumer behaviour.

Guilt is an advertising appeal that has been employed by organisations. For example, guilt appeals have been used by the UK government in their anti-smoking campaign which featured children asking their real mums and dads to stop smoking, appealing to the guilty consciences of the parents to change their behaviour (Anon, 2009). Charities are another sector which has used guilt appeals extensively. As one writer has noted, "a sad-eyed child with the tagline 'just three pounds can change a life', is a tactic used on a regular basis in non-profit marketing, from animal rights organisations to children's advocacy bodies" (Anon, 2009, p. 1).

Shock advertising is a route that was made infamous by Benetton, whose iconic shock appeal advertising ran for nearly two decades from 1982 to 2000. The photography-led campaign which the brand used over this period featured images which were designed to shock audiences, including a photograph of a real-life death scene (Attwell, 2013). Benetton's social issue-led campaign aimed to highlight key societal challenges at the time and was seen as highly controversial. However, shock advertising needs to be used cautiously and the ASA warns advertisers against using a "shocking claim" just to gain attention (ASA, 2013).

Other advertising appeals

There are a number of other types of appeal used by advertisers, such as celebrity appeals, expert appeals, slice-of-life, storytelling and sex appeals. Fill and Turnbull (2019) provide an overview of celebrity appeals and other spokespeople used in advertising, highlighting the value of using celebrities or experts in order to establish source credibility. The authors argue that using celebrities in advertising carries the risk that audiences may remember the celebrity in the advertising and not the brand (Fill and Turnbull, 2019, p. 610).

Advertising Brief **Celebrity appeals**

Using celebrities as spokespeople in advertising has been a popular route for advertisers in the last decade. For example, Emirates used Jennifer Aniston for their global advertising campaign which featured the Hollywood actress enjoying a flight on the airline's A380 aircraft. In addition to using celebrity actors, the airline has featured a number of sports celebrities in their films enjoying the in-flight services. As well as providing a strong testimonial for the brand, using celebrities allows campaigns to gain additional earned media for the campaign. However, advertisers need to ensure they choose their celebrity wisely to ensure there is a good fit between the brand and the celebrity.

Further reading

Erdogan, B. Z. (1999). Celebrity endorsement: A literature review. *Journal of Marketing Management, 15*(4), 291–314.

Neff, J. (2020, December 16). 12 smartest brand-celebrity pairings of 2020. *Adage*. Retrieved from https://adage.com/article/year-review/12-smartest-brand-celebrity-pairings-2020/2299341

Advertising which represents real life and shows consumers in real-life settings is known as slice-of-life. Using naturalistic contexts can be an effective way to connect with audiences since they are able to relate more easily with characters and settings that are familiar with their own real-life experiences. Slice-of-life often includes a storytelling element that shows characters within a plot. For example, the iconic "Gold Blend Couple" used this approach in a campaign which ran over seven years and featured the on/off romance between a couple. The advertising series became part of a national conversation and the final airing of the storyline attracted a television audience of 30 million.

Storytelling has been used in other settings and has become an increasingly popular route for advertisers over the last decade. The John Lewis Christmas campaigns, for example, have used a variety of characters to depict a Christmas story based around the brand's message of "thoughtful giving". In recent years, John Lewis have featured stories such as "Buster the Boxer", "Monty the Penguin" and a dragon called "Edgar", all of which have engaged audiences emotionally with the brand.

The use of sex appeals in advertising is controversial. However, many brands continue to use this route, especially in the perfume and aftershave categories. The main criticism of this route is that the advertising often objectifies men and women and this is seen to be harmful to society (Middleton et al., 2020). The ASA cautions advertisers that,

> "Whilst depicting people in a sexual way is not always offensive or problematic, Sexualisation and gratuitous nudity in ads can often cause serious or widespread harm and offence. Advertisers should avoid using sexualised imagery if this is irrelevant to the product, as this is likely to be considered offensive".
>
> (ASA, 2019, p. 1)

Advertising Brief   **Femvertising**

One new form of appeal that has appeared in recent years is femvertising. This type of appeal portrays women in advertising in more progressive ways, challenging the stereotypical portrayal of women traditionally seen in advertising. The term femvertising was first used by SHE Media in 2014 at Advertising Week New York and the organisation launched the first-ever #Femvertising Awards in 2015 to, "honor brands that are challenging gender norms by building stereotype-busting, pro-female messages and images into ads that target women and girls" (#Femverstising Awards, 2021).

Further reading

Åkestam, N., Rosengren, S., & Dahlen, M. (2017). Advertising "like a girl": Toward a better understanding of "femvertising" and its effects. *Psychology & Marketing, 34*(8), 795–806.

#Femvertising Awards (2021). *About the #Femvertising awards*. Retrieved from www.femvertisingawards.com/

References

Åkestam, N., Rosengren, S., & Dahlen, M. (2017). Advertising "like a girl": Toward a better understanding of "femvertising" and its effects. *Psychology & Marketing, 34*(8), 795–806.

Anon. (2009, December 8). The guilt appeal. *Marketing Week*. Retrieved from www.marketingweek.com/the-guilt-appeal/#:~:text=Search-,The%20guilt%20appeal,-Guilt%20marketing%20is

Anon. (2021). *Advertising standards authority*. Advertising guidance on depicting gender stereotypes likely to cause harm or serious or widespread offence. Retrieved from www.asa.org.uk/uploads/assets/6c98e678-8eb7-4f9f-8e5d99491382c665/guidance-on-depicting-gender-stereotypes.pdf

ASA. (2013, February 26). A quick guide to comparative advertising. *Advertising Standards Authority*. Retrieved from www.asa.org.uk/news/a-quick-guide-to-comparative-advertising.html

ASA. (2019, June 14). Offence: Sexualisation and objectification. *Advertising Standards Authority*. Retrieved from www.asa.org.uk/advice-online/offence-sexism.html

ASA. (2021, November 8). Fear and distress. *Advertising Standards Authority*. Retrieved from www.asa.org.uk/advice-online/fear-and-distress.html

Attwell, J. (2013, February 14). Alessandro Benetton on building a brand out of controversy. *Campaign*. Retrieved from www.campaignlive.co.uk/article/alessandro-benetton-building-brand-controversy/1170425

Darby, I. (2020, July 27). Advertising's fear factor: Marketing during a pandemic. *Campaign*. Retrieved from www.campaignlive.co.uk/article/advertisings-fear-factor-marketing-during-pandemic/1689289

Dumb Ways to Die website. Retrieved from www.dumbwaystodie.com/

Duracell. (2021). Retrieved from www.duracell.co.uk/help/bunny/

Erdogan, B. Z. (1999). Celebrity endorsement: A literature review. *Journal of Marketing Management, 15*(4), 291–314.

#Femvertising Awards. (2021). *About the #Femvertising awards*. Retrieved from www.femvertisingawards.com/

Fill, C., & Turnbull, S. (2019). *Marketing Communications: touchpoints, sharing and disruption*. Harlow: Pearson.

Kiefer, B. (2017, September 28). Audi sends in the clowns for big-budget tech campaign. *Campaign*. Retrieved from www.campaignlive.co.uk/article/audi-sends-clowns-big-budget-tech-campaign/1445813

Middleton, K., Thompson-Whiteside, H., Turnbull, S., & Fletcher-Brown, J. (2022). How consumers subvert advertising through rhetorical institutional work. *Psychology & Marketing, 39*(3), 634–646.

Middleton, K., Turnbull, S., & de Oliveira, M. J. (2020). Female role portrayals in Brazilian advertising: Are outdated cultural stereotypes preventing change? *International Journal of Advertising, 39*(5), 679–698.

Mulcahy, E. (2019, June 27). Humor marketing: Five ads that got consumers laughing. *The Drum*. Retrieved from www.thedrum.com/news/2019/06/27/humor-marketing-five-ads-got-consumers-laughing

Neff, J. (2020, December 16). 12 smartest brand-celebrity pairings of 2020. *Adage*. Retrieved from https://adage.com/article/year-review/12-smartest-brand-celebrity-pairings-2020/2299341

Sweney, M. (2013, June 22). Cannes Lions: Dumb ways to die scoops top award. *The Guardian*. Retrieved from www.theguardian.com/media/2013/jun/22/cannes-lions-advertising-awards

5 The creative development process

Learning outcomes

This chapter aims to enable readers to:

1 Explain what advertising creativity is
2 Understand the creative development process
3 Evaluate the stages in the process of creative development
4 Examine what makes advertising creative
5 Consider further reading on advertising creative development

What is creativity?

Creativity is one way to engage audiences. In a cluttered and fragmented media environment it is important that advertising stands out from other messages and captures the attention of audiences. Despite widespread recognition of the value attributed to creativity by clients and agencies, however, there is no agreed definition among advertising scholars or practitioners on what advertising creativity is (White and Smith, 2001). The lack of an agreed upon definition of creativity is not restricted to the advertising domain and has been a problematic area for creativity researchers in other settings (Amabile, 1996). Advertising scholars do agree, however, that advertising creativity does differ from creativity in the pure arts since advertising creativity has objectives set by the client (El-Murad and West, 2004). Despite a lack of a clear definition, there is some agreement that creative advertising should be original/novel and that it should be appropriate (Turnbull and Wheeler, 2017).

It is important to note that creativity is subjective and that what one person sees as being creative is not always viewed as creative by others. This may mean that clients may have a different view of creativity to their agency and even within agencies there may be differences between what a member

DOI: 10.4324/9781003175551-5

of the account services team views to be creative and what the art director or copywriter considers to be creative. These divergent views on creativity can create challenges within the creative development process. The Institute of Practitioners in Advertising (IPA) recognise how challenging it can be to judge creative ideas and have produced an industry guide to help advertisers evaluate creative work (IPA, 2021).

Advertising Brief   **What makes advertising creative?**

Choose a recent ad that you have seen on television, print or online which you think is creative. Try to judge for yourself if it is creative by answering the following questions:

- Is it original? Does it stand out from other ads in the same medium?
- Is it distinctive? Is it different from other ads in the same category?
- Is it appropriate? How relevant is it to the brand and to the target audience?

Further reading

West, D., Koslow, S., & Kilgour, M. (2019). Future directions for advertising creativity research. *Journal of Advertising*, *48*(1), 102–114.

Ensuring advertising is original is the key to the success of any campaign and it is also the most challenging aspect of developing creative work. Hurman (2016) argues that few advertising campaigns are creative and suggests that only one in every 7,000 campaigns would be considered creative enough to win an award. He cites Tony Davidson, the Creative Director of Wieden+Kennedy London, as arguing that, "great work should make you feel uncomfortable because it hasn't been done before" (Hurman, 2016, p. 42). Trying new approaches is likely to make the advertiser feel uncomfortable during the creative process and may make it hard for clients to judge creative work.

The creative development process

There are several distinct stages to the creative development process. Turnbull and Wheeler (2017) suggest there are 24 stages involved in creating ads within agencies and they provide a seven-stage model of the advertising creative process:

- Stage one: Task identification
- Stage two: Agreement of task objectives
- Stage three: Ideation
- Stage four: Response
- Stage five: Validation – internal
- Stage six: Validation – external
- Stage seven: Decision

Stage one: Task identification

This involves the identification that advertising is needed and can be the result of a brand review or a planned annual cycle. In most cases the advertiser will develop an advertising brief which will provide the agency with background information on the brand and an explanation of the campaign objectives, target audience and other considerations such as:

- Brand information: What are the brand's sales, market share and share-of-voice? Why is the campaign needed? What is the positioning of the brand in the market?
- Business objectives: What does the campaign hope to achieve? What are the business objectives? Are these objectives specific and measurable?
- Previous campaigns: What has the brand learnt from previous advertising campaigns? Which media works well? Which media has not performed well in the past for the brand? How have consumers responded to previous advertising?
- Communications objectives: What communication challenge does the campaign aim to address?
- Target audience: Who is the advertising targeting? Who is the primary and secondary target audience? What are the demographic, psychographic and geographic characteristics of the target audience? What are their media habits?
- Consumer insight: What key insights are known about the consumer and their buying habits? What does the customer journey look like?
- Single-minded proposition: What is the single most important message we wish to convey in the campaign?
- Tone of voice: What tone should be used to convey the message?
- Budget: How much is the overall advertising budget? What is the split between production and media?

- Campaign timing: What are the dates for the advertising? How long should the campaign run for? Are there any key dates that need to be considered i.e. new product launches?
- Mandatories: What are the essential elements that need to be included in the advertising? Does the message need to include a telephone number or website address? Does the advertising need to include a brand logo? Is there a strapline that needs to be included?

Advertising Brief   **How far will agencies go?**

The outdoor clothing brand Berghaus decided to send their advertising agency team to the top of a snowy mountain in the Lake District to pick up the brief for their next campaign (Fletcher, 1996). Why do you think Berghaus decided to ask the agency to do this? What aspects of the brief is the agency likely to understand better as a result of undertaking the mountain challenge? Consider other creative ways that Berghaus could brief their agency team in the future?

Further reading

Koslow, S., Sasser, S. L., & Riordan, E. A. (2006). Do marketers get the advertising they need or the advertising they deserve? Agency views of how clients influence creativity. *Journal of Advertising*, *35*(3), 81–101.

Stage two: Agreement of task objectives

Once the client has written the brief it is presented to the agency. This initial briefing meeting is usually attended by key client personnel and the agency team, including client services, account planners, media planners and the creative team. In some cases, this may be a standard meeting, although it is not unusual for some clients to arrange more interactive briefs. Turnbull and Wheeler (2017), for example, highlighted how one client hired actors to play the part of the target consumer to bring alive the consumer insight. The authors also explained how another client had taken the agency out on the River Thames on a speed boat to engage the agency with an exhilarating aspect of the brand. While not all clients employ such creative briefing experiences, they can provide a novel way to enthuse and engage the agency with the communication brief.

In most cases, once the agency has received the client brief, they will then translate the information into a creative brief. This is usually a single page document that is written into a standard agency creative brief template. The creative brief is an internal agency document and is discussed and agreed with the agency's creative director before being briefed into the creative team.

Stage three: Ideation

At this stage the creative ideas are developed by the creative team. Usually, creative teams are made up of an art director and a copywriter who work as a pair to interpret the brief and create ideas for the campaign. This may take days or weeks depending on the timing of the campaign and the scale of the brief. For new business pitches the creative team usually work to very short deadlines to create ideas and some agencies are known to set up "war rooms" to allow the creative teams to post their ideas onto the walls of the room as a reference point for the rest of the agency team.

Stage four: Response

Once the creative team have developed their ideas, they present their ideas to the agency's creative director. This stage may involve several rounds of revisions before the creative director approves the idea and agrees for concepts to be presented to the client.

Stage five: Validation – internal

The initial creative routes will be presented in a very rough format to the rest of the agency team to decide if the ideas meet the brief. If the ideas are considered to be on brief and are agreed by the agency team a meeting will be arranged to present them to the client.

Stage six: Validation – external

At this stage the ideas will be validated with the client. In many cases these initial creative ideas will be presented at a "tissue session" where possible creative routes and territories are shown as work in progress to the client to encourage feedback. The advantage of showing clients the creative work early on in the creative process is that it provides an opportunity for the client to validate the ideas at an early stage before the agency invests additional time and cost in developing work further.

If the client likes the initial ideas shared by the agency, they will consult their senior management and internal stakeholders to gain approval to proceed with the route. For global campaigns this may mean that clients seek feedback from their international markets.

Advertising Brief **Pre-testing**

Pre-testing ads with consumers in the right target audience is often used to help validate the creative route being taken. As well as ensuring that the creative idea resonates with the target audience, it can help the client and agency decide on the best route to take. Pre-testing is usually undertaken by a specialist research firm and increasingly, in an online format.

Further reading

Fill, C., & Turnbull, S. (2019). *Marketing Communications: touchpoints, sharing and disruption* (8th ed.). Pearson: Harlow.

Stage seven: Decision

Once the creative idea is approved by the client the creative idea usually goes into pre-testing. This may include both qualitative and quantitative research. In some cases where the client and agency have not agreed on the creative route, the pre-testing may be used to decide which creative idea will resonate with consumer. The testing allows the agency and client to check how consumers respond to the creative work before they invest in production costs and avoids the risk of running advertising that will be poorly received by the consumer. The pre-testing provides the agency with feedback to make refinements to the creative work and eliminate any routes that do not test well.

Advertising Brief **An agency view of the creative process**

There have been a limited number of studies which have explored how the creative development process works. Turnbull and Wheeler (2017) explore the stages within UK advertising agencies and highlight how agencies set up war rooms, and in some cases hold drive-by-briefs. Their study highlights the importance of validation and customisation within the creative stages.

Further reading

Turnbull, S., & Wheeler, C. (2017). The advertising creative process: A study of UK agencies. *Journal of Marketing Communications, 23*(2), 176–194.

References

Amabile, T. M. (1996). *Creativity in context*. Colorado: Westview Press.

El-Murad, J., & West, D. C. (2004). The definition and measurement of creativity: What do we know? *Journal of Advertising Research*, *44*(2), 188–201.

Fill, C., & Turnbull, S. (2019). *Marketing Communications: touchpoints, sharing and disruption* (8th ed.). Pearson: Harlow.

Fletcher, W. (1996, October 10). This week: Manchester advertising agency Cheetham Bell . . . . *Campaign*. Retrieved from www.campaignlive.co.uk/article/week-manchester-advertising-agency-cheetham-bell/54634

Hurman, J. (2016). *The case for creativity*. London: Cannes Lions.

IPA. (2021). *Judging creative ideas*. Retrieved from https://ipa.co.uk/knowledge/documents/judging-creative-ideas-best-practice-guide

Koslow, S., Sasser, S. L., & Riordan, E. A. (2006). Do marketers get the advertising they need or the advertising they deserve? Agency views of how clients influence creativity. *Journal of Advertising*, *35*(3), 81–101.

Turnbull, S., & Wheeler, C. (2017). The advertising creative process: A study of UK agencies. *Journal of Marketing Communications*, *23*(2), 176–194.

West, D., Koslow, S., & Kilgour, M. (2019). Future directions for advertising creativity research. *Journal of Advertising*, *48*(1), 102–114.

White, A., & Smith, B. L. (2001). Assessing advertising creativity using the creative product semantic scale. *Journal of Advertising Research*, *41*(6), 27–34.

6 International advertising

Learning outcomes

This chapter aims to enable readers to:

1 Understand the challenges of advertising in international markets
2 Examine the advantages of advertising standardisation
3 Discuss the advantages of a localised approach to advertising
4 Evaluate the cultural considerations when advertising internationally
5 Consider further reading on international advertising

Advertising in international markets

There are a number of considerations that advertisers need to take into account when planning and implementing campaigns in international markets. One key factor is culture, and advertising needs to understand the cultural values and societal norms of their audience. Culture relates to all aspects of consumers lives and helps to explain how society works and how members of the society communicate with each other. Without a good understanding of these societal norms and the cultural attitudes and beliefs, advertising is unlikely to resonate with consumers.

There are many aspects of culture and language. Both verbal and non-verbal language are important factors that provide rich insights into how societies socially interact. Language can be symbolic and can highlight the importance that communities attach to relationships, family attachments, age, gender and time. Advertising needs to ensure that the language used in advertising messages is aligned to cultural values. The increase in global campaigns designed to run across multiple territories has resulted in more advertising using music and less copy or voice-overs, avoiding any language issues.

DOI: 10.4324/9781003175551-6

Advertising also needs to consider how language is written. Languages such as Arabic, for example, are written right to left which means consumers view content starting on the right. The Middle East also attaches great cultural value to the use of calligraphy, and thus the way in which the Arabic language is written has important symbolism in the region.

Advertising Brief **Brief: Lost in translation**

Brands need to consider the subtle nuances of language when advertising in different cultures to their home market. If a translation of the advertising isn't correct the message can have a very different meaning than the one originally intended by the brand. Munro (2019, p. 1), for example, provides the case of Parker Pen's launch campaign in Mexico which mistranslated the word "embarrass" into "embarzar", meaning "impregnate" in Spanish. This meant that rather than Parker Pen's advertising proposition claiming that their pens, "won't leak in your pocket and embarrass you", it instead suggested, "It won't leak in your pocket and impregnate you" (Munro, 2019, p. 1).

Further reading

Manco, C. (2020, July 8). Keep it local. *WARC.* Retrieved from www.warc.com/newsandopinion/opinion/keep-it-local/3718
Munro, G. (2019, July). How brands can localise their visual content strategy at a global scale. *WARC.* Retrieved from www.warc.com/content/article/bestprac/how-brands-can-localise-their-visual-content-strategy-at-a-global-scale/127197

Non-verbal language also needs to be considered when developing international advertising and brands need to choose imagery that is appropriate for the local culture. Melewar et al. (2000), for example, highlight how Middle East advertisers should avoid some imagery and suggest that advertising avoids showing statues which can be interpreted as a form of idolatry in local culture. The authors also argue that colour is important in Middle East culture and explain how one brand decided not to run their global advertising showing purple silk because purple is seen as the colour of death.. Munro (2019) highlights colour as a key consideration when choosing imagery and explains that while the colour orange has warm connotations in Western cultures, in the Middle East orange is seen as a sign of loss or mourning. Munro (2019, p. 1) suggests that, "It is important to research different colour meanings – it is almost impossible to find colours that have universal meanings, so this would commonly need to be altered when visuals are localised".

Advertising Brief   **Wise old owl**

Some images have symbolic importance in local culture. For example, it is not uncommon in Middle East advertising to see images of camels and falcons, which are traditional and as such have cultural significance. Munro (2019) highlights the need to consider the appropriateness of visual metaphors when selecting imagery for advertising and provides the example of the owl, which in Europe and North America is seen as symbol of knowledge and wisdom, but in some cultures represents death and witchcraft.

Further reading

Melewar, T. C., Turnbull, S., & Balabanis, G. (2000). International advertising strategies of multinational enterprises in the Middle East. *International Journal of Advertising, 19*(4), 529–547.

In addition to factors such as language and imagery there are other cultural factors that advertising should consider, including:

- Manners and customs: What are the local customs that should be observed? What holidays are celebrated in the country? What is considered polite in the culture? What would be considered rude? For example, in the Middle East it is considered impolite to show the sole of your foot.
- Education: What is the level of education in the country? What are the levels of literacy in the market?
- Religion: What are the religious beliefs in the country? What are the ethical values linked to religion? What practices might be considered inappropriate or offensive to religious beliefs?
- Economic: What is the state of the country's economy? How much disposable income do consumers have in the market? What economic restriction or challenges are there in the market?

- Technological: What technology is available to consumers in the country? What media do consumers have access to? What are consumers' media habits and preferences?
- Legal: What are the legal restrictions for advertising in the country? What other laws impact advertising in the market?
- Regulatory: What are the advertising regulations in the country? What are the specific regulatory restrictions that apply to the brand category?

While this chapter has so far highlighted the differences that exist between cultures, some scholars argue that there is a global consumer culture and that brands are able to tap into universal values. Alden et al. (1999) proposed the concept of global consumer culture positioning (GCCP), which suggests that there are globally shared meanings which brands can use to strengthen their brand equity.

Standardise or localise?

Since Theodore Levitt suggested that all markets are similar and that consumers around the world have the same needs and desires as each other, there has been an ongoing debate about whether global advertising should be standardised (Levitt, 1993). While there is no strict definition of what constitutes standardised advertising, it is widely accepted that this is seen to be advertising where all elements of the message with the exception of the copy remain unchanged. Advocates of standardising advertising suggest it provides a number of benefits to the brand and the consumer including:

- Consistent brand image: Having the same messages and images in every country provides global synergy in the advertising. Not only will consumers around the world see the same messages, but consumers travelling to other countries will see the same messaging and imagery in each country they visit.
- Economies of scale: Both in terms of productions costs and media buying. This means that content can be created centrally and then shared globally for use in each market. While it is likely that some translation of messages will be undertaken, the production costs will be cheaper than developing new campaign ideas for each different country. Consolidating advertising budget could allow more funds to be allocated to production costs and hence encourages more ambitious creative ideas.
- Planning and control: Having a standardised approach allows for greater control over advertising in all markets. There is less risk that markets will create campaigns that are not aligned to the brands vision or out of keeping with the brand's tone of voice.

- Global media planning and buying: With some media offering access to global audiences, including social media platforms, a centralised approach means that advertisers can plan and book media to reach consumers around the world.

Advertising Brief **Advertising in the Arab Middle East**

The decision of whether to standardise or localise advertising in the Arab Middle East has been a challenge for practitioners for decades. As well as the media availability and language issues, there are cultural beliefs and religious values that need to be considered when developing advertising for the region. In particular, Turnbull et al. (2016) highlight the importance of considering Islamic ethics when developing advertising for the Arab Middle East and suggest that practitioners observe unity (*Tawheed*), faith (*Iman*), trusteeship (*Khilafah*), balance, justice or adl and free will. They suggest that comparative advertising is less desirable and that advertisers need to ensure the imagery used in advertising is culturally appropriate.

Further reading

Turnbull, S., Howe-Walsh, L., & Boulanouar, A. (2016). The advertising standardisation debate revisited. *Journal of Islamic Marketing*, *7*(1), 2–14.

In contrast to the standardised approach, many scholars and practitioners argue in favour of adopting a localised strategy. Brands that adopt a localised strategy will adapt their advertising messages in each market to take local culture and taste into consideration. A localised approach is seen to have a number of advantages:

- Respects local culture: This means that the advertising is created to appeal to local culture and lifestyles and is therefore likely to resonate with audiences more than standardised messages produced for a global consumer.
- Ability to respond to local market conditions: Localised advertising can be used to respond to particular local market needs such as competitor activity or address localised consumer needs.
- Appropriate for local market advertising regulations: Most countries have their own industry regulations and advertising guidelines. Developing advertising within each market ensures local practices and legislation is taken into consideration.

- Media infrastructure: A localised approach allows for campaigns to be developed around the most effective media for the market. In Saudi Arabia, for example, cinemas were banned until 2018 when it was announced that a 35-year ban would be lifted (Kinninmont, 2018). A localised approach would provide an opportunity to consider the particular strengths and weaknesses of media availability and usage in the local market during the campaign development stage.

While some authors argue that adaptation is a more effective route (de Mooij and Hofstede, 2010), in practice most brands use a mix of strategies depending on the local market. For some, a "glocalised" approach, mixing the benefits of each strategy, is considered the most practical. A "glocal" approach might see a global creative strategy and creative platform used in all markets to provide a consistent feel to the advertising, but language and imagery adapted to meet the needs of local market.

 **Snickers global strategy with local application**

Snickers's global campaign, "You're Not You When You're Hungry", is a good example of how a global strategy can be used internationally and adapted to suit local markets. The Snickers campaign, which has run in a number of countries, including Australia, France, the United Kingdom and the United Arab Emirates, tapped into a global truth that humans are bad tempered when they are hungry and adapted the messaging to suit local cultures. The agency teams were given guidelines to ensure that the advertising tone of voice remained consistent wherever the advertising appeared to provide synergy. Local creative teams built campaigns reflecting national values and customs. For example, in China the Snickers campaign tapped into the cultural experience of high school students preparing for the very long national *gaokao* exam (Whiteside, 2020).

Further reading

Whiteside, S. (2020, October 29). Effectiveness insights from ten years of Snickers' "You're not you when you're hungry". *WARC*. Retrieved from www.warc.com/newsandopinion/opinion/effectiveness-insights-from-ten-years-of-snickers-youre-not-you-when-youre-hungry/3892

de Mooij, M., & Hofstede, G. (2010) The Hofstede model. *International Journal of Advertising*, 29(1), 85–110.

References

Alden, D. L., Steenkamp, J. B. E., & Batra, R. (1999). Brand positioning through advertising in Asia, North America, and Europe: The role of global consumer culture. *Journal of Marketing*, *63*(1), 75–87.

de Mooij, M., & Hofstede, G. (2010). The Hofstede model. *International Journal of Advertising*, *29*(1), 85–110.

Kinninmont, J. (2018, April 17). Saudi Arabia: Why is going to the cinema suddenly OK? *BBC News*. Retrieved from www.bbc.co.uk/news/world-middle-east-43738718

Levitt, T. (1993). The globalization of markets. *Readings in International Business: A Decision Approach*, *249*, 249–252.

Manco, C. (2020, July 8). Keep it local. *Warc*. Retrieved from www.warc.com/news andopinion/opinion/keep-it-local/3718

Melewar, T. C., Turnbull, S., & Balabanis, G. (2000). International advertising strategies of multinational enterprises in the Middle East. *International Journal of Advertising*, *19*(4), 529–547.

Munro, G. (2019, July). How brands can localise their visual content strategy at a global scale. *Warc Best Practice*. Retrieved from www.warc.com/content/article/bestprac/how-brands-can-localise-their-visual-content-strategy-at-a-global-scale/127197

Turnbull, S., Howe-Walsh, L., & Boulanouar, A. (2016). The advertising standardisation debate revisited. *Journal of Islamic Marketing*, *7*(1), 2–14.

Whiteside, S. (2020, October 29). Effectiveness insights from ten years of Snickers' "You're not you when you're hungry". *Warc*. Retrieved from www.warc.com/newsandopinion/opinion/effectiveness-insights-from-ten-years-of-snickers-youre-not-you-when-youre-hungry/3892

7 Media

Learning outcomes

This chapter aims to enable readers to:

1 Understand the media landscape
2 Examine the media channels available to advertisers
3 Evaluate paid, owned and earned media
4 Discuss the main advantages and disadvantages of each channel
5 Consider further reading on media

The media landscape

The last two decades has seen a transformation in the media landscape. New technology has created new forms of media and new opportunities, spaces and places to communicate with audiences. While technology and behaviourial changes have brought about new opportunities for advertisers, they have also presented new challenges. Audiences are using media when mobile and multitasking across channels. Furthermore, the increase in media channels has meant that audiences are fragmented and it is harder than ever before to reach them.

The media landscape is divided into three types of media, commonly referred to as POE:

- Paid: This refers to any type of media which requires payment by the advertiser to place their message. For example, television, newspapers, radio, paid ads within online games and Facebook ads.
- Owned: This is media that the brand has control of and therefore does not require payment for placing advertising. For example, a brand's own website.

DOI: 10.4324/9781003175551-7

- Earned: This refers to media such as word of mouth or conversations on social media platforms that mention the brand. For example, a conversation on Twitter about a brand. It also includes media coverage earned on TV or in press.

The industry also refers to 'Shared Media' which is seen as a strategy to drive the sharing of messages through social media.

Media channels and cross-platform campaigns

In practice, most advertising uses a mix of POE media depending on the campaign objectives and budget. While the number of media channels has increased dramatically over the last 20 years, advertisers need to consider the strengths of each channel in their planning. There is a large amount of data and research available to media planners to help them in their planning decisions, including the Joint Industries Currencies, which were created to provide objective trading metrics for each media channel and to help advertisers and agencies evaluate the effectiveness of cross-platform campaigns (BARB, 2021).

Television

Television has always been a powerful media channel and this remains true in today's media landscape. A study undertaken by the Institute of Practitioners in Advertising (IPA) identified that campaigns which include television are significantly more effective than campaigns without it (Binet and Field, 2017). The IPA study identified that television in particular is the biggest driver of market share and that brands that use television increase market share twice as fast as those that do not (Binet and Field, 2017). Thus, television is still seen as a lead media channel.

The strength of television may in part be explained by the volume of TV ads watched by TV audiences. Whereas consumers may choose to use ad blockers and skip ads on digital platforms, a 2020 study by Thinkbox, the marketing body for commercial television in the United Kingdom, identified that 68% of TV viewers watched over 50 ads a week (Thinkbox, 2021). This demonstrates the potential reach that television offers advertisers.

Advertisers can book advertising spots of various lengths on television, although traditionally 30-second and 60-second spots, lasting for 30 seconds and 60 seconds respectively, remain the most popular lengths. Television can be booked for short spot lengths, such as a 10-second or 20-second spots. These shorter lengths can be used to support longer ads and provide an opportunity to extend the life of a campaign. There is also the opportunity to run blipverts which are very short ads lasting around two seconds and usually used as a teaser to create excitement around a new product or a launch (Thinkbox, 2021). Often advertisers run five blipverts in one commercial break which makes the equivalent of one ten-second spot.

As well as short lengths, television can be used for 90-second-plus spots. While these longer spots are obviously more expensive, the advantage of running longer ads is that they are more likely to dominate the ad break. These long form spots are often used to launch a campaign and are then supported by shorter spots on television or on digital platforms such as Facebook or YouTube to extend the life of a campaign (Thinkbox, 2021). Broadcasters also offer opportunities to run themed breaks which last several minutes.

Advertising Brief | **Live ads**

Using live TV ads is one way for advertisers to capture the attention of audiences. The use of live ads can drive audience responses in real-time and although a risky option for advertisers, they have become increasingly popular. For example, Honda used a live TV ad showing their skydiving team jump 14,000 feet over Spain in a Channel 4 ad break. The ad, called "Jump", saw skydivers fall from an aircraft at 300 mph and lasted 3 minutes and 20 seconds during which time the skydivers spelt out "Honda" (Sandison, 2008).

Waitrose's "Spring" campaign also featured a live TV ad. Although arguably not as high risk as the Honda stunt, it was nevertheless a first for TV advertising. The TV ad featured a live stream from a GoPro camera fitted to a cow in a field to raise awareness of the welfare of the animals on Waitrose farms (Oakes, 2016).

Further reading

Sandison, N. (2008, May 29). Honda to create history with live skydiving ad. *Campaign*. Retrieved from www.campaignlive.co.uk/article/honda-create-history-live-skydiving-ad/812557

Oakes, O. (2016, April 12). Waitrose to stream live ad from dairy farm. *Campaign*. Retrieved from www.campaignlive.co.uk/article/waitrose-stream-live-ad-dairy-farm/1390748

Radio

Radio offers a number of advantages to media planners. One distinct benefit is that radio is listened to in a variety of contexts, meaning that audiences may be listening to advertising while travelling to school or eating lunch. Radio is also a relatively cheap channel, and as well as the cost of the spots themselves, radio ads can be produced at low cost. Furthermore, the production of radio ads is quick, making them a good choice for short-term tactical campaigns.

Radio is often referred to as "theatre of the mind" since it has the ability to conjure the imagination of audiences through sound. This provides distinct advantages to advertisers who are able to create vivid pictures in the minds of listeners using sound alone. For example, using sounds of waves and seagulls will instantly transport listeners to the seaside and conjure up images of beaches and summer. This unique aspect of radio provides greater scope for creativity.

Regan (2016, p. 1) identifies the main advantages of radio as a media channel as follows:

- Ubiquity and reach: Widespread reach to consumers in a variety of contexts.
- Targeting: The variety of stations allows for targeting by geographic, demographic and lifestyle factors.
- Brand affinity: Radio stations and shows often have loyal audiences and have built a community that can benefit the advertiser.
- Recency: Advertising messages can be delivered at the point of consumer decision making, whether this be at home or on the way to the shops.
- Topicality/creative flexibility: Allows for seasonal campaigns. Radio is broadcast every day of the year for 24 hours a day and this provides opportunities for advertisers to tailor campaigns to reflect the time of the day or special calendar events.
- Cost: Radio advertising is relatively low cost and therefore affordable for brands with smaller advertising budgets.
- Secondary channel: Radio is a good support media channel and works well as part of a multimedia advertising campaign.

Newspapers

This channel is defined as, "online and offline publishing platforms of national and regional newspapers, both paid for and free" (Gibbs, 2017,

p. 1). While some newsbrands have seen decreases in advertising spend in recent years, especially regional newsbrands, others have retained their advertising income by providing additional multimedia opportunities.

In the same way that television offers mass reach, so too do newspapers. Gibbs (2017) argues that newsbrands offer significant scale for advertisers, allowing 47 million consumers to be reached across print and online platforms. Gibbs (2017) also highlights how newspapers can "supercharge" other media and reports on findings of a Newsworks/Benchmarketing study which suggests that print newsbrands double the effectiveness of TV media spend. Furthermore, he argues that the study identified print newsbrands boost online display and video by up to four times and radio revenue up to ten times (Gibbs, 2017). These findings recognise the value that newsbrands can have within an advertising campaign.

WARC (2019a) highlights three current trends in newspaper advertising that are seen to be effective. The first is the use of paid newspaper partnerships where brands are working with newspapers to provide content that is relevant to the readers. For example, Gillette deodorant sponsored content on the front pages and used inserts within Orthodox newspapers in Israel to reach the Orthodox Jewish community (WARC, 2019). Second, brands are using newspapers to gain earned media for culturally relevant campaigns. For example, Nando's ran pull-outs in newspapers in Washington DC in the run up to the presidential inauguration that doubled as campaign posters. Third, newspapers are still used as an effective channel to reach mass target audiences. For example, Pampers used newspaper advertising in India to reach young mothers to educate them about the hygiene advantages of using disposable nappies (WARC, 2019a).

Magazines

In the same way that newspapers have evolved into multi-platform media over the last decade, so too have magazines. As well as the printed version of magazines, many titles offer digital editions, social media and other opportunities for advertisers to engage with magazine readers on specific topics of interest. Cloete (2017, p. 1) argues that the multi-platform offering and the focus on content means this channel can be defined as, "professionally edited, original content that focuses on a particular passion point shared by the brand and the reader".

Many magazines offer advertisers access to consumers with specialist interests which means that readers have an affinity with the magazine and are more likely to be engaged with content that is relevant to them.

Magazines also provide the opportunity for advertisers to reach consumers with a specific demographic profile. For example, Dubai Properties wanted to reach ultra-high-net-worth property buyers to attract investment in their Jumeirah Beach Residences 1/JBR development and used magazines within their campaign (WARC, 2019). Magazines were chosen as they were seen to allow the advertiser access to these elite consumers in a high-quality context.

Magazines offer a high-quality reproduction of ads and this is an advantage to brands which want their ads to reflect the quality of their products or services. Additionally, magazines are seen to have an extended life because they may be read by more than one person. However, magazines often have long booking lead times and therefore may be less suitable for use within short-term activation campaigns.

Cinema

Cinema is a media channel that allows advertisers to reach audiences in an environment that is free of distraction and in a context where they are emotionally engaged with the content (WARC, 2021). Although many cinemas have been impacted by closures during the Covid-19 crisis and the delay in the release of some blockbuster films, cinema advertising is expected to see ad spend levels return to normal levels post pandemic.

Cinema offers an immersive context which means that audiences are more receptive to advertising messages. A trip to the cinema is a leisure activity and therefore advertisers can benefit from the enjoyment audiences are experiencing when they go to see a film. There are also opportunities to schedule advertising that is relevant to the particular film being shown to heighten audience engagement.

A further advantage of this channel is that many cinemas are located in town centres and therefore near to shops. This provides "recency", meaning that advertising can be delivered in a location near to a purchase decision. There are also opportunities for regional buying and therefore cinema ads can be shown in locations near to retailers' outlets or car showrooms. For example, Wagamama used cinemas in locations near to their restaurants and scheduled spots around the time that audiences were most likely to eat after they had seen the film, which drove short-term sales for the restaurant chain (WARC, 2020).

Similar to radio, cinema is a channel that is often seen as a support channel, especially for television. WARC (2021) argues that cinema is particularly effective at extending the life of a TV campaign and has the advantage that the same content can be used for both television and cinema.

 **How Audi used cinema to address gender stereotypes**

Audi saw cinemas as a perfect context for storytelling and used this channel to address gender stereotypes. The car manufacturer created a 30-second animated feminist fairy tale called "Ever After" which was showed over 4,000 times in cinemas across Spain over the Christmas holidays (WARC, 2019). The animated film was scheduled to run before films such as *Star Wars: The Last Jedi* (2017) and *Coco* (2017). Running the ad over the Christmas period and alongside family movies meant that more families were exposed to the gender equality message.

Further reading

Audi Spain Ever After (2018). *WARC*. Retrieved from www.warc.com/content/article/Audi_Spain_Ever_After/123782
WARC (2019b). What's working in Cinema. *WARC*. Retrieved from www.warc.com/content/article/warc-wwi/whats-working-in-cinema/129302

Out-of-home (OOH)

Out-of-home (OOH) or outdoor includes a wide variety of different media channels, including roadside billboards, bus stop panels and advertising on transport. It also includes other spaces that are available to advertisers such as beer mats, shopping trolleys, petrol pumps and point-of-sale.

Advertisers can also take advantage of opportunities in digital out-of-home (DOOH). For example, British Airways created the "Magic of Flying" digital billboard for London's Piccadilly Circus. The digital billboard used custom built technology to track aircraft and when a British Airways flight was passing overhead, other brand advertising was interrupted to show an image of a child pointing skywards and revealing the British Airways flight number and the destination that the plane was coming from (de la Fosse, 2021). Passersby were encouraged to #lookup and watch the British Airways aircraft fly past. This demonstrates the creative opportunities that DOOH offers advertisers to engage audiences.

Digital out-of-home can also be used interactively. The MicroLoan Foundation used DOOH as part of their "Pennies for Life" campaign to increase donations for small business loans to women in Africa. Every time viewers texted a £2 donation the poster site refreshed to show pennies falling onto the screen to make up the face of an African women smiling. Similarly, the charity Compassion in World Farming used DOOH interactively, allowing viewers to feed pigs on a farm when they made a donation (Anon, 2014).

Advertising Brief   ## Women's Aid "Look at Me"

To mark International Women's Day, the charity Women's Aid created an interactive DOOH to raise awareness of domestic violence. The screens used the attention of people to change the images shown. Using facial detection technology and gaze tracking the interactive billboards were able to recognise when viewers were looking at the screen. As people stopped to look at the image of a women's face covered with bruises this was detected by the software and the bruises on the face of the woman started to heal in real-time. This interactive creative supported a clear campaign message that taking notice can help women suffering from domestic violence (Anon, 2015).

Further reading

Anon (2015, March 5). Women's Aid and Ocean amplify the violent face of abuse with the world's first visually powered DOOH campaign. *Ocean*. Retrieved from https://oceanoutdoor.com/ocean-news/case-studies/womens-aid-and-ocean-amplify-the-violent-face-of-abuse-with-the-worlds-first-visually-powered-dooh-campaign/

Digital channels

Digital channels include a range of paid, owned and earned media. Paid media includes media such as; paid social, paid ads in search, video on demand, promoted Tweets, Facebook ads, in-app advertising, banners and online display. Digital channels also include owned media such as a brand's own website or microsite, branded social media messages, hosted videos on YouTube and advertising on a branded app. Earned media includes social media conversations that are shared and news coverage on television or other media. This means that some of the previous channels already discussed in this chapter can also be included within category. For example, coverage received from a TV news network online.

Digital channels are seen to offer very distinct advantages to advertisers and afford a range of opportunities that allow for engagement with consumers. Feldwick (2018) highlights five key advantages that digital channels offer:

- Immediacy: Offering advertisers an opportunity to respond to comments or issues as they arise.
- Intimacy: Advertisers can interact directly with consumers. There is also scope for personalisation.
- Interactivity: Advertisers can engage with consumers directly.
- Immersive: Provides opportunities to create engaging experiences for consumers.
- Innovative: Allows opportunities for advertisers to use novel creative routes.

The Internet Advertising Bureau (IAB, 2021) highlights that advertisers need to consider the quality of their advertising if they want to engage audiences in digital channels. The IAB argue that advertisers need to ensure that digital advertising observes the following rules:

- Relevance: Ensure the advertising is relevant to audiences.
- Blend well: Advertising should blend in to the environment in which they are served.
- Good production standards: Advertising should be creative and well produced.
- Authentic: Advertising should be transparent.
- Do not interrupt: Advertising should not intrude on the consumer's digital experience.

This guidance offered by the IAB highlights the importance for advertisers to recognise the distinct characteristics of digital channels. While digital advertising provides opportunities for creative flexibility and allows advertising to be delivered at critical decision-making moments in the customer journey, advertisers need to respect the consumer's digital space.

 **"Don't Mind If I Baileys"**

Bailey's used digital display and mobile display as part of their campaign to re-energise the brand and serve advertising to audiences at times and in places when they were most likely to treat themselves. Digital display delivered treat recipes to consumers at work and at home at times when they were thinking about indulging in a treat. Mobile display was used to target audiences when shopping in the supermarket and delivered relevant creative messages. The campaign also used recipe videos delivered through social media sites. Digital channels worked effectively to support television and enabled messages to be delivered at consumer decision points, aligning with a recency media planning strategy (Mackay-Sinclair et al., 2018).

Further reading

Mackay-Sinclair, K., Farrelly, J., & Thomson, J. (2018). Baileys: A radical brand turnaround story with extra sprinkles. *WARC*. Institute of Practitioners in Advertising, Silver, IPA Effectiveness Awards. Retrieved from www.warc.com/content/article/baileys-a-radical-brand-turnaround-story-with-extra-sprinkles/122381#:~:text=Baileys%3A%20A%20radical,Effectiveness%20Awards%2C%202018

References

Anon. (2014, March 27). Brands rise to the creative challenge of DOOH. *Campaign.* www.campaignlive.co.uk/article/brands-rise-creative-challenge-dooh/1287228

Anon. (2015, March 5). Women's aid and ocean amplify the violent face of abuse with the world's first visually powered DOOH campaign. *Ocean.* Retrieved from https://oceanoutdoor.com/ocean-news/case-studies/womens-aid-and-ocean-amplify-the-violent-face-of-abuse-with-the-worlds-first-visually-powered-dooh-campaign/

Audi Spain Ever After. (2018). *Warc.* Retrieved from www.warc.com/content/article/Audi_Spain_Ever_After/123782

Barb. (2021). *Joint industry currencies.* Retrieved from www.barb.co.uk/about-us/joint-industry-currencies/

Binet, L., & Field, P. (2017). *Media in focus: Marketing effectiveness in the digital era.* London: IPA.

Cloete, M. (2017, July). How to use magazines effectively in the media mix. *WARC Best Practice.* Retrieved from www.warc.com/content/article/bestprac/how-to-use-magazines-effectively-in-the-media-mix/111764 de la Fosse, E. (2021, April 13). My campaign: The making of British Airways "The magic of flying". *Campaign*. Retrieved from www.campaignlive.co.uk/article/campaign-making-british-airways-the-magic-flying/1712366

Feldwick, O. (2018, April). How digital channels can help build a brand. *WARC Best Practice*. Retrieved from www.warc.com/content/article/bestprac/how-digital-channels-can-help-build-a-brand/121367

Gibbs, I. (2017, March). How to plan an effective newspaper campaign. *Warc Best Practice*. Retrieved from www.warc.com/content/article/bestprac/how-to-plan-an-effective-newspaper-campaign/110508

IAB. (2020, December 16). Five rules to ensure the quality of your digital advertising. *IAB*. Retrieved from www.iabuk.com/research/five-rules-ensure-quality-your-digital-advertising

Mackay-Sinclair, K., Farrelly, J., & Thomson, J. (2018). Baileys: A radical brand turnaround story with extra sprinkles. *Warc*. Institute of Practitioners in Advertising, Silver, IPA Effectiveness Awards. Retrieved from www.warc.com/content/article/baileys-a-radical-brand-turnaround-story-with-extra-sprinkles/122381#:~:text=Baileys%3A%20A%20radical,Effectiveness%20Awards%2C%202018

Oakes, O. (2016, April 12). Waitrose to stream live ad from dairy farm. *Campaign*. Retrieved from www.campaignlive.co.uk/article/waitrose-stream-live-ad-dairy-farm/1390748

Regan, T. (2016, September). How to plan an effective radio campaign. *WARC Best Practice*. Retrieved from www.warc.com/content/article/bestprac/how-to-plan-an-effective-radio-campaign/108928

Sandison, N. (2008, May 29). Honda to create history with live skydiving ad. *Campaign*. Retrieved from www.campaignlive.co.uk/article/honda-create-history-live-skydiving-ad/812557

Thinkbox. (2021, May 4). Introduction to spot advertising. *Thinkbox*. Retrieved from www.thinkbox.tv/how-to-use-tv/spots/introduction-to-spot-advertising/

Warc. (2019a, January 19). What's working in newspapers. *Warc Category Intelligence*. Retrieved from www.warc.com/content/article/warc-wwi/whats-working-in-newspapers/124777

Warc. (2019b). *What's working in cinema*. Retrieved from www.warc.com/content/article/warc-wwi/whats-working-in-cinema/129302

Warc. (2020). Stirring souls and selling bowls the wagamama way, through the secret power of cinema. Institute of Practitioners in Advertising, Bronze, IPA Effectiveness Awards. Retrieved from www.warc.com/content/article/stirring-souls-and-selling-bowls-the-wagamama-way-through-the-secret-power-of-cinema/133196

Warc. (2021, March). What we know about cinema advertising. *WARC Best Practice*. Retrieved from www.warc.com/content/article/bestprac/what-we-know-about-cinema-advertising/110495

8 Media planning

Learning outcomes

This chapter aims to enable readers to:

1   Understand the challenges of media planning
2   Examine the influences on media planning
3   Evaluate the principles and ethical issues related to media planning
4   Discuss media planning calculations
5   Consider further reading on media planning

Media planning challenges

The media landscape has undergone significant changes over the last 20 years and new technology and changes in consumer media viewing habits have greatly influenced media planning decisions.

In addition to the increase in media channels there has been a proliferation of data generated, particularly from consumers' digital behaviour. As a result, media planners have access to large amounts of data from research, media owners, third party suppliers and their own agency media planning tools. The increase in the volume of and complexity of data has led to many agencies creating roles for data planners to manage and interpret the data for clients.

 **Programmatic advertising**

Programmatic advertising is defined as, "the use of algorithm-driven software to replace humans in the purchase and delivery of adverts on a variety of online platforms with the opportunity to show an ad to a

DOI: 10.4324/9781003175551-8

specific customer, in a specific context" (Charlesworth, 2021, p. 61). Programmatic advertising was initially created to sell empty online advertising space and it now accounts for about half of all online advertising (Charlesworth, 2021).

Further reading

Charlesworth, A. (2021). *Absolute essentials of digital marketing*. Oxon: Routledge.

Influences on media planning

Media planning decisions are influences by a number of factors. One of the key factors to consider is the campaign objectives which need to provide media planners with clear direction on the aims of the advertising. For example, if the campaign is required to drive short term uplift in sales, then channels which are better at activation will be selected. However, if the campaign objectives are to build brand share longer term, then channels such as television, which is commonly used for brand building, will be targeted.

Channel choices however depend on the media budget available. For example, while it might meet the campaign objectives to plan television, there may not however be sufficient budget to support using this channel. As well as being expensive in terms of media costs, there are also high production costs involved which may make television unaffordable for some advertisers.

Planners will also need to consider the customer journey and how consumers make purchase decisions. Planners will need to understand who the target audience are and the touchpoints along the customer journey where consumers can be reached. It is important to identify the best point along the journey to target them since the timing of the delivery is key. Advertisers should also take the context of where the message is being delivered into account.

Other factors that need to be considered are seasonality. For example, ice cream sales are more likely during hot weather and therefore ice cream brands are likely to schedule their advertising during the warm summer months. Equally, seasonal factors such as key holiday periods when consumers are more likely to purchase gifts or go on holiday may be relevant for other advertisers.

The product life cycle is a further consideration. New products, for example, usually require advertising to raise awareness of the product launch and grow initial market share. After launch, advertising is usually required to maintain or grow share of market and will be influenced by competitive advertising activity in the category.

The creative idea will also influence the channel selection. Creativity should not be seen as the exclusive responsibility of the creative team, as media planners are also able to explore creative ways to use media and new media opportunities. For example, Turnbull (2018) highlights how the Ministry of Public Health in the Islamic Republic of Afghanistan chose a creative medium to deliver their health message. The Ministry used charm bracelets as part of their campaign to improve awareness of vaccinations among infants in the country which has low literacy rates. The "Immunity Charm" campaign chose the bracelets to ensure the message reached communities targeted.

Advertising Brief   **Hot enough for an ice cream?**

Wall's ice creams ran a campaign on OOH, DOOH, mobile, Facebook and Twitter featuring talking ice creams. The creative featured a range of executions that were made relevant to the place, event or weather. Since the brand had a limited media budget, 80% of the media spend was thermally activated (Carter, 2018). This meant that the ads only ran when the temperature got warm enough to trigger the consumer's appetite for an ice cream. The campaign also used geo-targeting so that advertising was delivered in places close to where consumers could buy ice creams.

Further reading

Carter, S. (2018, April 18). Why Wall's made its classic ice-creams talk. *Campaign*. Retrieved from www.campaignlive.co.uk/article/why-walls-made-its-classic-ice-creams-talk/1462374

The principles of media planning

There are a number of key principles that apply to media planning, including reach, frequency, recency, effective cover and context. Media planners are expected to consider each of these when they are selecting channels to ensure that they use media budgets in the most cost effective and efficient manner.

- Reach: Total percentage of the target audience that will be reached.
- Frequency: This is the number of times the target audience will be exposed to the advertising.

- Recency: Refers to the closeness of the message to the point of purchase.
- Effective cover: The number of times the target audience need to be exposed to the message to be effective.
- Context: The environment in which the message will be delivered.

The effective frequency concept in media planning suggests that, "for nearly all products there exists an optimal number of advertising exposures below which no or little effect is observed, and above which advertising effectiveness demonstrates diminishing return" (Makienko, 2012, p. 58). Although there has been much debate regarding the effectiveness concept and many advertisers have interpreted effective frequency as meaning running an ad "three-plus" times, Makienko (2012) identified that advertisers use levels of five to six exposures, with some choosing to run 12.

The concept of recency was introduced by Ephron (1997) and challenges the concept of effective frequency. Ephron (1997) argues that recency is more important because it is based on when consumers are ready to buy, rather than how many times the message should reach audiences. He argues that the, "goal is to place a brand message close to a purchase" (Ephron, 1997, p. 7). Recency planning has become increasingly used in a digital era where advertisers are able to reach consumers in a wider range of contexts, including while mobile.

 **How This Girl Can reached audiences with Spotify**

This Girl Can and MediaCom teamed up with Spotify to devise a novel way to target women who were not keeping up with their physical exercise routine. Insight identified that many women exercise to a playlist, and by partnering with Spotify, This Girl Can was able to identify who had not been listening to their exercise playlists for more than 30 days. Those that had not were shown a This Girl Can message to inspire them to start exercising again. This novel targeting reached 250,000 women and the results showed that 49% of the women acted upon the message.

Further reading

Anon (2018, January 24). The clever way that This Girl Can and Media-Com used Spotify to get women moving. *Campaign*. Retrieved from www.campaignlive.co.uk/article/clever-girl-mediacom-used-spotify-women-moving/1450564

Media planning calculations

There are a number of basic calculations used by media planners, including:

- Television rating (TVR): Measures the popularity of a TV programme.
- Cost per thousand (CPT): Calculates the cost of reaching 1000 people in a brand's target audience.
- Gross rating points (GRPs): Calculates the coverage by the average frequency.
- Share of voice (SOV): The share of advertising in comparison to competitors.

Advertising Brief   ## Share of Google searches

Binet (2020, p. 1) introduced a new metric called "share of searches", which is defined as, "the share of organic Google search queries (not share of paid search advertising) and the metric equates to total searches for a specific brand, divided by the total searches for all brands in that category". Binet (2020) argues that this new metric is an effective measure for tracking relative interest in a brand compared to other brands in the same category, and share or search correlates with market share.

Further reading

Binet (2020). Binet presents fast, cheap, predictive share of search metric. *IPA website*. Retrieved from https://ipa.co.uk/news/binet-presents-fast-cheap-predictive-share-of-search-metric

---

Ethical media planning

Media planners should consider the ethical implications of their planning decisions. The Conscious Ad Network (2021) highlights the main ethical considerations media planners need to be aware of when making media choices:

- Ad fraud: Agencies are encouraged to educate their employees about the risks of ad fraud and ensure they have policies in place to identify ad fraud. Agencies are encouraged to support anti-fraud initiatives and ensure they are certified for the Joint Industry Committee for Web Standards

(JICWEBS) anti-fraud initiatives (Ad Fraud, 2019).The JICWEBS anti-fraud initiatives support the US Trustworthy Accountability Group (TAG) programme, which is a global initiative to eradicate fraudulent web traffic, combat malware and prevent internet piracy (TAG, 2019).

- Diversity: Advertisers are encouraged to fund diverse media titles and ensure that brand safety settings are not excluding media that represents diverse audiences. Advertisers should also be cautious about targeting audiences on protected characteristics (Diversity in Content, 2020).
- Informed consent: Advertisers should be respectful of online audiences and be transparent about how personal data is being collected, stored and used. In line with General Data Protection Regulation (GDPR), advertisers should ensure that they meet the obligations of informed consent regarding personal data access and handling (Informed Consent, n/d).
- Hate speech: Advertisers should, "Endeavour to avoid advertising with media outlets that fuel hatred on the grounds of race, religion, nationality, migration status, sexuality, gender or gender identity, disability or any other group characteristic" (Hate Speech, n/d, p. 1).
- Children's wellbeing: Advertisers should ensure that advertising is age appropriate and the impact of the advertising on children's wellbeing should be taken into consideration (Children's Wellbeing, n/d).
- Mis/disinformation: Advertisers should avoid advertising in media which, "commercialise inaccuracies, distort facts, and do not clearly label opinion and conjecture, harass individuals, peddle rumours, hoaxes and conspiracy for commercial gain, or which promote misinformation about climate science or public health. And report to local regulators, the publications or platforms that do" (Mis/Disinformation, 2021, p. 1).

Advertising Brief **The media ecosystem**

Fill and Turnbull (2019) provide a comprehensive review of media planning in a digital age. They outline how media planners view the interdependencies between channels and the role of the characteristics of a media ecosystem. The authors provide an overview of a schematic used by media planners to ensure media budgets are maximised across paid and owned media.

Further reading

Fill, C., & Turnbull, S. (2019). *Marketing Communications: touchpoints, sharing and disruption*. Harlow: Pearson.

References

Ad Fraud. (2019). *Conscious ad network*. Retrieved from www.consciousad network.com/manifestos/antifraud.pdf

Anon. (2018, January 24). The clever way that This Girl Can and MediaCom used Spotify to get women moving. *Campaign*. Retrieved from www.campaignlive. co.uk/article/clever-girl-mediacom-used-spotify-women-moving/1450564

Binet. (2020). Binet presents fast, cheap, predictive share of search metric. *IPA Website*. Retrieved from https://ipa.co.uk/news/binet-presents-fast-cheap-predictive-share-of-search-metric

Carter, S. (2018, April 18). Why Wall's made its classic ice-creams talk. *Campaign*. Retrieved from www.campaignlive.co.uk/article/why-walls-made-its-classic-ice-creams-talk/1462374

Charlesworth, A. (2021). *Absolute essentials of digital marketing*. Oxon: Routledge.

Children's Wellbeing. (n/d). *Conscious ad network*. Retrieved from www.consciousadnetwork.com/manifestos/children_wellbeing.pdf

Conscious Ad Network. (2021). *Our six manifestos*. Retrieved from www.consciousadnetwork.com/#Manifestos

Diversity in Content. (2020). *Conscious ad network*. Retrieved from www.consciousadnetwork.com/manifestos/diversity.pdf

Ephron, E. (1997). Recency planning. *Journal of Advertising Research*, *37*(4), 61–66.

Fill, C., & Turnbull, S. (2019). *Marketing Communications: touchpoints, sharing and disruption*. UK, Harlow: Pearson.

Hate Speech. (n/d). *Conscious ad network*. Retrieved from www.consciousad network.com/manifestos/hate_speech.pdf

Informed Consent. (n/d). *Conscious ad network*. Retrieved from www.conscious adnetwork.com/manifestos/informed_consent.pdf

Makienko, I. (2012). Effective frequency estimates in local media planning practice. *Journal of Targeting, Measurement and Analysis for Marketing*, *20*(1), 57–65.

Mis/Disinformation. (n/d). *Conscious ad network*. Retrieved from www.consciousadnetwork.com/manifestos/CAN_Mis_Disinformation_V2_Apr_2021.pdf

TAG. (2019). *TAG certified against fraud guidelines*. Retrieved from https://cdn2.hubspot.net/hubfs/2848641/TAG%20Certified%20Against%20Fraud%20Guidelines%20v4.0_FINAL.pdf

Turnbull, S. (2018). Using labels and accessories as creative advertising media: Insights from Cannes Lions 2017. *Current Trends in Fashion Technology & Textile Engineering*, *3*(2), 555606.

9   Advertising measurement and metrics

Learning outcomes

This chapter aims to enable readers to:

1   Examine why advertising is measured
2   Understand testing during campaign development
3   Evaluate campaign monitoring and optimisation
4   Discuss measurement of post-campaign results
5   Consider further reading on advertising measurement and metrics

Why measure advertising?

Measurement is an important aspect of any advertising campaign and the measures should be considered as part of the initial campaign planning and included in any brief. There are three main stages of an advertising campaign that advertisers may wish to evaluate:

- Campaign development: Creative ideas may be evaluated to decide which is the most appropriate or which strategy is more likely to achieve the required objectives.
- Campaign monitoring and optimisation: Monitoring campaigns as they run and evaluating how audiences are engaging with campaigns allows advertisers to optimise performance.
- Post-campaign results: Advertisers will measure whether the campaign has met the objectives they set out to achieve. This allows for advertisers to evaluate the return on their campaign investment.

Measurement allows advertisers to evaluate what worked in a campaign and to determine aspects of the advertising that did not perform as well as intended. This information provides valuable learnings for future campaigns

DOI: 10.4324/9781003175551-9

and allows advertisers to develop their own internal benchmarks for measurement to help with future decision making.

Campaign development

In many cases, advertisers will test initial creative ideas with consumers as part of the creative development process. Known as "copy testing" or "pretesting", this involves the evaluation of the creative ideas before they go into production and can also be used to fine tune creative executions after production and before the ads are launched in the media. Copy testing helps to ensure that the idea resonates with audiences and that the intended message is clear. In some cases, more than one idea is tested with consumers to see which route is preferred and to decide which executions are likely to be most effective.

There are a variety of reasons why advertisers use copy testing. Poole (2016) argues that copy testing works best when it is used to maximise return on investment and when the sample used in the research is representative of the target audience. He identifies five key advantages of copy testing:

- Improves opportunities to achieve greater return on investment for the brand.
- Provides a check to ensure the original creative idea has not been lost in the creative development process.
- Provides an opportunity to check the response of the target audience.
- Demonstrates the likely sales effect of the creative.
- Provides confidence to use a brave creative route.

Although there are distinct advantages to copy testing, measuring creative effectiveness at concept stage is not without its critics. One of the main concerns levied at copy testing is that it can dismiss really good ideas at an early stage. Critics also argue that copy testing does not take place in a real setting and therefore results may be misleading. Although not all creative ideas are copy tested, many advertisers see this as a safety net and have developed their own testing benchmarks for their brand.

Copy testing is seen to allow advertisers an opportunity to measure the creative idea for a number of factors (Poole, 2016) including:

- Engagement: This may include likeability or emotional response to the advertising.
- Ad recall: Determine how memorable the advertising is.
- Strength of brand: Identify if the advertising has strong branding.
- Brand messaging: What the advertising says about the brand.

- Brand outcomes: Measures likely short and long-term impact of the advertising.
- Viral potential: Provides an indication of the potential of the advertising to be shared.

The process of pre-testing involves drawing up ideas into concept boards which are presented to a sample of the target audience. Focus groups have been a traditional means of copy testing and use qualitative measures to evaluate concepts. Quantitative techniques are also used and a number of online proprietary tools that include self-aided interviews have been developed which allow testing results to be delivered to advertisers within hours.

Advertising Brief **Neuroscience techniques**

Neuroscience techniques offer an alternative solution to measuring the effectiveness of advertising. Harris et al. (2018) identify a range of neuroscience techniques that can be used to measure physiological responses to advertising. They outline which techniques are appropriate for marketing research and suggest that a number of techniques are suitable for advertising including;

- Electroencephalography (EEG): Measures the frequency of the brain's electrical currents.
- Eye tracking: Measures eye movements.
- Heart rate (ECG): Measures heart rate.
- Galvanic skin response (GSR): Measures the skin's sweat response.

Further reading

Harris, J. M., Ciorciari, J., & Gountas, J. (2018). Consumer neuroscience for marketing researchers. *Journal of Consumer Behaviour*, *17*(3), 239–252.

Campaign monitoring and optimisation

In addition to optimising creative ideas prior to a campaign launch, advertisers also need to ensure that they evaluate the in-market performance of their advertising. This is often undertaken using ad tracking research, and data is collected using consumer surveys.

Ad tracking studies measure audience attitudes towards the advertising message in a real world setting and thus provides a valid measure of whether the advertising is performing as planned in market. IPSOS (2016, p. 1) argues that ad tracking is valuable for advertisers,

> "without such insight, it is hard for clients to understand what to do differently or better going forward. Is the advertising capturing consumer attention (recall, recognition, and correct brand attribution), and having an impact on behaviour (i.e., sales) or brand desire (i.e., equity or imagery)".

IPSOS (2016) suggests that ad tracking offers a number of distinct advantages:

- Verifies that the pre-test works in a real world setting.
- Allows assessment of impact of advertising on brand objectives.
- Permits ad wearout to be monitored.
- Allows identification of the competitors response to the advertising.
- Provides data for review on media scheduling.

Tracking studies can also provide valuable information on the performance of the media mix. This information can be used to adjust the channel mix in future campaigns. It is also important to monitor and optimise media budgets during a campaign. This allows changes to be made to media plans while the campaign is still running. This is especially true of a digital media campaign where advertisers use a dashboard to monitor activity using key metrics.

Advertising Brief | **Market mix modelling**

Market mix modelling is a statistical technique using multiple regression techniques which allows advertisers to optimise the mix of marketing channels and tools used in a campaign. The modelling uses previous campaign data to forecast the impact of the mix being planned and then adjusts as necessary in order to optimise effectiveness.

Further reading

Neilsen. (2021) Market mix modelling. *Neilsen Website*. Retrieved from www.nielsen.com/uk/en/solutions/capabilities/marketing-mix-modeling/

Metrics are important measures of digital advertising campaigns. Hanlon (2019) argues there is a clear distinction between measures and metrics and highlights how metrics should be seen as performance measures that need to be reviewed regularly. She highlights the importance of regular reviews of how digital campaigns are performing to understand what is working and what is not working, allowing for changes to be made to a campaign. The dashboard provides a means to monitor and evaluate digital campaigns.

There has been much criticism around the choice of metrics used to measure digital advertising. A key concern has been on the use of "vanity measures" and the real effect of a campaign can be distorted by "fake" followers and "likes" which may not accurately reflect the engagement with the advertising. Another criticism has been the overreliance on the use of the "click" which was one of the first metrics used to measure engagement with digital advertising.

Despite criticism of existing metrics, it is common for advertisers to use the dashboards provided by the channels which provide a range of metrics for campaigns, including "likes" and "follows". As well as the dashboards provided by individual channels, there are many commercial software systems that provide dashboards for monitoring digital advertising.

Advertising Brief **Twitter metrics**

Dashboards are used to measure the level of activity and allow analysis of campaigns on Twitter. The Tweet activity dashboard is a free service offered to Twitter users that provides brands with a range of metrics to help evaluate the effectiveness of a campaign such as number of impressions and engagement rates with content. Twitter (2021, p. 1) identifies the most common metrics used to evaluate campaigns:

- App install attempts
- App opens
- Detail expands
- Embedded media clicks
- Engagements
- Engagement rate
- Likes
- Follows
- Hashtag clicks
- Impressions

- Link clicks
- Permalink clicks
- Replies
- Retweets
- Shared via email
- User profile clicks

Source: Twitter. (2021). Tweet and video activity dashboards. *Twitter Website.* Retrieved from https://business.twitter.com/en/help/campaign-measurement-and-analytics/tweet-activity-dashboard.html

Further reading

Fulgoni, G. M. (2016). In the digital world, not everything that can be measured matters: How to distinguish "valuable" from "nice to know" among measures of consumer engagement. *Journal of Advertising Research,* *56*(1), 9–13.

Post-campaign results

How campaign outcomes are measured depends largely on the strategy and objectives set during the planning stage. For example, if a campaign's objectives are to increase visitors to a website, then the increase in the numbers of visitors to the site could be used to evaluate whether this objective has been met or not. However, advertisers need to consider other factors that might have contributed to website traffic. A celebrity or influencer might have posted a comment about the website and this may have influenced the increase in number of visitors. This example highlights the challenge of attributing outcomes to specific advertising activity.

As discussed, tracking studies can provide valuable insights on the impact of the advertising and highlight which channels have performed well during the campaign. Tracking studies allow advertisers to see the impact of the campaign on brand awareness, ad awareness and brand response. A tracking study will also inform advertisers on how the advertising message resonated with audiences and to what extent the message stood out in a cluttered media environment.

Other methods that are used are econometric modelling techniques which employ regression analysis to isolate factors that influence a dependent variable such as sales. Cook (2014, p. 1) outlines the advantages of using modelling techniques in advertising and argues that,

> "Econometric modelling allows us to determine how movements in sales or other brand KPIs come about. Were they driven by communications,

price, weather or some other factor? As we build a model, we identify the key drivers and quantify their impacts over both the short and longer term. For communications, this is enormously helpful. It allows us to determine how much each media channel contributes and over what timescale. It can also help us identify threshold spend levels at which communication is becoming less effective pound for pound".

Econometrics is seen as a valuable measurement of effectiveness and many advertisers use specialist services to evaluate advertising using this technique.

Binet and Field (2007) recommend using econometrics whenever possible to measure the financial return of advertising and to ensure that all factors are taken into account when evaluating advertising effectiveness. The authors argue that the main objective of any commercial campaign is profit and highlight the importance of using hard business measures over behavioural measures when measuring advertising. Binet and Field (2007) suggest advertisers use a balanced scorecard using multiple measures, including factors such as share price and investors' ratings, rather than a single metric when evaluating the effectiveness of advertising.

| *Advertising Brief* | **Using emojis to measure engagement** |

Turnbull and Jenkins (2016) suggest that emojis could be one way to overcome the challenge of measuring audience engagement with campaigns on social media. Their paper considers the problematic nature of social media metrics and concerns around "vanity measures" and "fake" followers and suggest using emojis to evaluate how audiences engage with campaigns on digital platforms. In particular, Turnbull and Jenkins (2016) discuss using Facebook reactions, which provide a means to analyse consumer engagement on a number of emotional dimensions, including:

- Love (love)
- Haha (amusement)
- Yay (happiness)
- Wow (surprise)
- Sad (sadness)
- Angry (anger)

The authors suggest that Facebook reactions provides a way to evaluate emotional engagement with social media campaigns in a more effective way than other metrics.

Further reading

Turnbull, S., & Jenkins, S. (2016). Why Facebook reactions are good news for evaluating social media campaigns. *Journal of Direct, Data, and Digital Marketing Practice*, *17*(3), 156–158.

References

Binet, L., & Field, P. (2007). *Marketing in the era of accountability identifying the marketing practices and metrics that truly increase profitability*. IPA. Retrieved from https://ipa.co.uk/knowledge/publications-reports/marketing-in-the-era-of-accountability

Cook, L. (2014, February). Econometrics: Get the best from econometric modelling. *Admap*. Retrieved from www.warc.com/content/article/A101109_Econometrics_Get_the_best_from_econometric_modelling/101109

Fulgoni, G. M. (2016). In the digital world, not everything that can be measured matters: How to distinguish "valuable" from "nice to know" among measures of consumer engagement. *Journal of Advertising Research*, *56*(1), 9–13.

Hanlon, A. (2019). *Digital marketing: Strategic planning & integration*. London: Sage.

Harris, J. M., Ciorciari, J., & Gountas, J. (2018). Consumer neuroscience for marketing researchers. *Journal of Consumer Behaviour*, *17*(3), 239–252.

IPSOS. (2016). Ipsos encyclopedia: Advertising tracking research. *IPSOS*. Retrieved from www.ipsos.com/en/ipsos-encyclopedia-advertising-tracking-research

Neilsen. (2021). Market mix modelling. *Neilsen Website*. Retrieved from www.nielsen.com/uk/en/solutions/capabilities/marketing-mix-modeling/

Poole, D. (2016, June). How to use copy testing or pre-testing. *Warc Best Practice*. Retrieved from www.warc.com/content/article/bestprac/how-to-use-copy-testing-or-pre-testing/107800

Turnbull, S., & Jenkins, S. (2016). Why Facebook reactions are good news for evaluating social media campaigns. *Journal of Direct, Data, and Digital Marketing Practice*, *17*(3), 156–158.

Twitter. (2021). Tweet and video activity dashboards. *Twitter Website*. Retrieved from https://business.twitter.com/en/help/campaign-measurement-and-analytics/tweet-activity-dashboard.html

10 Advertising

Industry structure and practice

Learning outcomes

This chapter aims to enable readers to:

1 Understand the structure of the industry
2 Examine the difference between in-house and agency models
3 Evaluate the different types of advertising agency
4 Discuss agency holding groups and key industry issues
5 Consider further reading on advertising industry practice

Industry structure

The industry is structured around three key groups (Fill and Turnbull, 2019); The advertiser (who pays for the advertising), the advertising agency (who is hired by the advertiser to develop and plan the campaign) and the media owner (who owns the space or time where the advertiser wishes to place their advertising). Each one of these has an important role within the industry.

- Advertiser: This is the brand owner who funds the advertising. Examples include John Lewis, Emirates and Heinz.
- Advertising agency: This may be a creative, media, integrated or specialist agency that is working with the advertiser to develop, plan and book a campaign. Examples include adam&eveDDB, Grey and McCann Erickson.
- Media owner: This is the organisation which owns the media and will charge for space or time. Examples include Channel 4, The Times and Instagram.

In recent years, with the advent of digital and social media channels, the boundaries between the role of the agency and media owner has become

DOI: 10.4324/9781003175551-10

less well defined. It is not unusual, for example, to see owners of digital platforms working directly with advertisers without the direct involvement of advertising agencies.

Digital platforms and big data have also disrupted traditional agency services and structures and as a result there has been considerable growth over the last decade in specialist digital agencies. Furthermore, advancements in Internet of Things (IoT) are blurring the boundaries of what constitute "media" and this is likely to disrupt the structure of the industry even further in the future.

In-house or external advertising agency?

A key decision for many advertisers is the choice of whether to use an external advertising agency or to undertake the roles performed by an agency in-house. In part, this may be determined by the size of the organisation and the advertising expertise they have in the company.

Using an external advertising agency can provide a number of distinct advantages, including objectivity and access to a wider skill set. However, there are also distinct benefits from using an in-house agency and there has been a rising trend in the number of organisations that are using in-house agencies. Pepsi, for example, set up an in-house agency called the Creators League in 2016 to create branded and un-branded content, including scripts, music recordings and films (Schultz, 2018). One advantage for Pepsi, like many other brands which have created their own in-house agency, has been the ability to develop content for digital platforms very quickly. This aspect of speed is an important consideration for organisations, and this, together with the ability to have greater control over advertising, makes the in-house option attractive for many advertisers.

The in-house agency model is not a new one and there have been some brands which have been developing their own advertising for decades. Specsavers in the UK, for example, has been producing their own advertising since 1985. However, the in-house option is not without its critics. While having an in-house agency may result in fewer delays, managing an in-house agency has implications for fixed costs and can distract an organisation from its core business activity. There is, however, a third option available for advertisers which is an on-site agency. This allows an external agency network to set up a bespoke agency within the advertiser's offices. These on-site agencies have the benefits of an in-house agency model, offering proximity and speed, as well as the advantages of an external agency such as objectivity. Examples of this agency model include the McDonald's We Are Unlimited agency in Chicago.

Many advertisers do use a mix of models and it not uncommon to see organisations using external advertising agencies for strategy and campaign development and having an in-house agency to support the development and produce support materials. Fill and Turnbull (2019) provide a comprehensive overview of the advantages and disadvantages of choosing an external agency and the selection process. They highlight the importance for agencies of creative awards such as Cannes Lions in attracting new clients.

Advertising **Agency-client relationships**

There have been several studies over the last four decades that have explored the relationship between advertisers and agencies. Some client-agency relationships have lasted more than 30 years and marriage analogies are not uncommon when describing partnerships between and advertising agency and client (Turnbull, 2016). In many cases close friendships form between the client and agency personnel (Turnbull and Wheeler, 2009).

Agency-client relationships can be seen as having different stages. Turnbull (2016) identifies five stages through which the client/ad agency relationship develop: Pre-relationship, early relationship/ pitch, transition, development and maintenance and dissatisfaction. The author argues that the relationships should be seen as transitionary and that although some working agreements may end, clients and agencies may continue their relationship.

Turnbull and Wheeler (2016) have explored what clients look for in an agency partnership and identify that clients hire agencies for their "craft" and access to their creative talent. However, the study also highlights the importance that advertisers attribute to the relationship between themselves and their agency. The findings show that clients look for agencies with whom they share chemistry, and the authors argue that, "Advertisers want to feel an affinity towards the advertising agency they select" (Turnbull and Wheeler, 2016, p. 54).

Further reading

Fill, C., & Turnbull, S. (2019). *Marketing Communications: touchpoints, sharing and disruption*. Pearson: Harlow.

Turnbull, S., & Wheeler, C. (2016) Exploring advertiser's expectations of advertising agency services. *Journal of Marketing Communications*, *22*(6), 587–601.doi: 10.1080/13527266.2014.920902

Turnbull, S. (2016). From pitch to ditch: The client/ad agency life cycle. *The Marketing Review*, *16*(2), 111–127.

Types of agencies

Just as there is a mix of agency models, there is also a variety of advertising agency types. These range from the large integrated agencies offering a full range of services to small boutique agencies that have particular areas of specialisation, such as creative or digital. The Institute of Practitioners in Advertising (IPA) highlight the different types of service that agencies provide and identify four main areas of expertise (IPA, 2021a):

- Strategic services such as strategic brand planning and research.
- Design services such as graphic design, video and user experience.
- Technology services such as data management and engineering.
- Advertising services such as creative development, media planning and buying, public relations, direct marketing.

There are currently six main types of agencies which exist, offering a variety of services. However, it should be stressed that just as new agencies have emerged to service digital advertising needs and social media requirements, it is inevitable that new agency types will appear in the future to service advertising technologies of the future. The current types of agencies have been categorised by the IPA (2021a) as:

- Integrated "full-service" agency: This agency offers a full service to advertisers including strategic planning, campaign development and media planning and booking. Such agencies will also offer clients digital and social media planning and management, public relations, search engine optimisation (SEO) and research.
- Digital agency: This agency type specialises in digital advertising and offers clients expertise in areas such as SEO, social media campaigns, email marketing and website design.
- Social media agency: This agency specialises in social media services such as content creation and optimisation for social media channels.
- Brand agency: This agency provides brand services such as brand identity and logo design.
- Creative agency: This agency specialises in creativity and offers expertise in creative development.
- Media planning and buying agency: This agency provides media planning and media buying expertise. They will plan and book media space on behalf of the advertiser.

While each of the agencies offer different specialist services to advertisers it is worth noting that the origination of a campaign idea is not the exclusive responsibility of an integrated or creative agency. In some cases, for example, it is the media agency that will take the lead and use data driven insights to generate the "big idea".

 **Working in an advertising agency**

There are a variety of roles within agencies, including account planning, media planning and buying, finance, human resource management and creative service roles. There are also roles for client services personnel whose job it is to liaise between the client and agency teams and co-ordinate the progress of the client's work within the agency. The client services person is commonly referred to as a "suit" within the agency and many advertising agencies offer trainee schemes for this role. Working in client services requires good interpersonal communication skills as the role demands managing the relationships between the clients and the agency.

Turnbull (2019) highlights some of the desirable skills that advertising agencies seek when hiring graduate students into agency roles. She argues that critical thinking, analytical and problem-solving skills as well as an appreciation of the wider challenges facing society are all valuable attributes.

Further reading

Turnbull, S. (2019). Lessons from the United Kingdom: Employability, brand responsibility, and a nation of "ad lovers". *Journal of Advertising Education*, *23*(2), 140–143.

IPA. (2021b). Careers in advertising. *IPA*. Retrieved from https://ipa.co.uk/knowledge/careers-in-advertising

---

Agency holding groups

It is important to recognise that many agencies are owned by the same holding groups. There are several very large groups which control many of the world's biggest agency networks, and as a result have responsibility for much of the advertising revenue globally. The top ten groups as identified by revenue generated by Statista (2021) in ranked order are:

- WPP London ($16.9 million)
- Omnicom Group, New York ($15 million)
- Publicis Groupe, Paris ($12.3 million)
- Accenture Interactive, New York ($10.3 million)

- Interpublic Group of Cos, New York ($10.2 million)
- Dentsu Group Inc., Tokyo ($9.6 million)
- Deloitte's Deloitte Digital, New York ($7.9 million)
- PwC's PwC Digital Services, New York ($6.7 million)
- IBM Corp.'s iX, Armonk, New York ($5.6 million)
- BlueFocus Communication Group, Beijing ($4.1 million)

The list highlights the increasing share of management consultancy firms in the advertising agency space and demonstrates the opportunities for a wider range of organisations to compete with traditional agencies for advertising revenue. The list of top ten agencies also reflects the global nature of the industry and the dominance of holding companies in the sector based in the United States.

These large holding groups and their international agency networks wield considerable power over the advertising industry globally. Given the power of advertising to shape society, these holding groups have a moral responsibility to ensure that advertising is conducted in an ethical manner. As well as consideration for the advertising campaigns being socially responsible, holding companies need to act responsibly towards their employees.

Advertising   **Women in adland**

The advertising industry has faced growing criticism over the last decade for the lack of diversity in creative departments. In particular, the lack of women in senior creative roles has been a topic of much debate in adland and there have been numerous studies exploring the challenges that woman face. Thompson-Whiteside et al. (2020) identify the gendered nature of creative departments and the challenges that creative women face when working in a male dominated environment. In their 2021 study, Thompson-Whiteside and Turnbull examine how women in French advertising agencies used their communication skills to expose sexual harassment within French advertising.

Further reading

Thompson-Whiteside, H., & Turnbull, S. (2021). #Metoovertising: The institutional work of creative women who are looking to change the rules of the advertising game. *Journal of Marketing Management*, *37*(1–2), 117–143.

Thompson-Whiteside, H., Turnbull, S., & Howe-Walsh, L. (2020). Advertising: Should creative women be expected to 'fake it?'. *Journal of Marketing Management*, 1–26.

Industry leadership on inclusivity and diversity

A number of research studies have identified the gendered practices that exist within advertising creative departments (Thompson-Whiteside et al., 2020; Thompson-Whiteside and Turnbull, 2021). These have highlighted the need for advertising leaders to address the wider issues of diversity, inclusion and equity in the industry (Conscious Advertising Network, 2020, p. 1). Organisations such as the Conscious Advertising Network argue that, "At board level, all leaders should be accountable for driving diversity throughout the DNA of their brand and business". The call for greater diversity has led to a census of advertising and the creation of a new directory to encourage diverse talent into the industry (All In Directory, 2021).

 **All In Census**

In March 2021, three key advertising bodies, Advertising Association, the IPA and Incorporated Society of British Advertisers (ISBA) collaborated to undertake an "All In Census", providing the largest ever survey of inclusion and diversity in the UK advertising industry. The results of the census were published in the *All In Action Plan* and highlighted that, "Generally, we are seeing reasonable representation across each of the diversity characteristics with social mobility and disability being the two areas that need focus. Older age groups are also under represented when compared to the UK working population. However, the picture changes when we look at C-suite representation with most minority groups under-represented, in particular women, Black, Asian and disabled employee populations" (All In Directory, 2021, p. 10).

To address the issues identified in the census, the industry bodies have worked together to establish the *All In Action Plan* and set up the *All In Directory* which provides resources to support and encourage the recruitment of diverse talent into advertising. The directory is a useful source of information for anyone wanting to find out more about opportunities in the industry.

Further reading

All in Directory. (2021): https://adassoc.org.uk/all-in/directory/

In addition to recent initiatives such as the All In Census, which highlights agency initiatives to address inclusion and diversity, The Conscious Advertising Network (2020) has asked brands to challenge their agencies on diversity issues. The network argues that there is a commercial imperative to widen the recruitment pool at entry level and provides a list of questions for advertisers to evaluate levels of inclusion and diversity within their agency (Conscious Advertising Network, 2020).

Advertising   **A question of ethics**

The Conscious Advertising Network (2020) suggests that brands ask a number of questions of their agencies to challenge existing logics. They list 12 questions that should be posed by brands (Conscious Advertising Network, 2020, p. 1):

1   Does the agency you're working with have a commitment to inclusion and diversity? What is their vision/mission for this and how does it show up as part of their agency ethos?
2   What is representation like at board/C-suite/throughout the business?
3   What is your agency's gender pay gap? Disability pay gap?
4   Are they accredited with the Creative + Media Equality Standard from Creative Equals?
5   Have you considered your own bias in research and strategy?
6   Is the creative brief reflective of the audience you want to reach?
7   What is the representation of the teams working on the brief?
8   Is your agency aware of the ASA gender stereotyping standards set in 2019?
9   Have you outlined requirements for inclusive work (including accessibility)?
10   What will representation look like on screen and behind the screen?
11   What are the agency's supply chain commitments? Will the production chain be diverse and inclusive (are they signed up to Free the Work)? How will the work be cast?
12   Where will your ads be served? Which sites are you supporting? Is your media play inclusive, whether this is online or OOH?

Further reading

Advertising Standards Authority (2020, August 13). *Harm and Offense: gender stereotypes*. Retrieved from www.asa.org.uk/advice-online/harm-and-offence-gender-stereotypes.html

Conscious Advertising Network. (2020): www.consciousadnetwork.com/manifestos/diversity.pdf

Creative Equals: www.creativeequals.org/

Free The Work: https://freethework.com/

References

All in Directory. (2021). Retrieved from https://adassoc.org.uk/all-in/directory/

Conscious Advertising Network. (2020). *Diversity in content*. Retrieved from www. consciousadnetwork.com/manifestos/diversity.pdf

Fill, C., & Turnbull, S. (2019). *Marketing Communications: touchpoints, sharing and disruption*. Harlow: Pearson.

IPA. (2021a). Agency sizes, structures, departments and salaries. *IPA Website*. Retrieved from https://ipa.co.uk/knowledge/careers-in-advertising/agency-sizes-structures-departments-and-salaries

IPA. (2021b). *Careers in advertising*. Retrieved from https://ipa.co.uk/knowledge/careers-in-advertising

Schultz, E. J. (2018, April 26). Pepsico eyes outside investors for its creators league. *AdAge*. Retrieved from https://adage.com/article/cmo-strategy/pepsico-eyes-investors-creators-league-studio/313272

Statista. (2021). *Leading advertising agency groups worldwide in 2019, by revenue*. Retrieved from www.statista.com/statistics/273879/revenue-of-the-worlds-largest-agency-companies/

Thompson-Whiteside, H., & Turnbull, S. (2021). # Metoovertising: The institutional work of creative women who are looking to change the rules of the advertising game. *Journal of Marketing Management, 37*(1–2), 117–143.

Thompson-Whiteside, H., Turnbull, S., & Howe-Walsh, L. (2020). Advertising: Should creative women be expected to "fake it?". *Journal of Marketing Management*, 1–26.

Turnbull, S. (2016). From pitch to ditch: The client/ad agency life cycle. *The Marketing Review, 16*(2), 111–127.

Turnbull, S. (2019). Lessons from the United Kingdom: Employability, brand responsibility, and a nation of "ad lovers". *Journal of Advertising Education, 23*(2), 140–143.

Turnbull, S., & Wheeler, C. (2009, September). Business friendships: A free lunch? Or a source of competitive advantage. In *International Conference on Managerial Solutions for the Global and Local Markets: Management of Marketing, Human Resources, Innovation, and Finance during a Crises*, Nessebar, Bulgaria, pp. 9–12.

Turnbull, S., & Wheeler, C. (2016). Exploring advertiser's expectations of advertising agency services. *Journal of Marketing Communications, 22*(6), 587–601. doi: 10.1080/13527266.2014.920902

Index

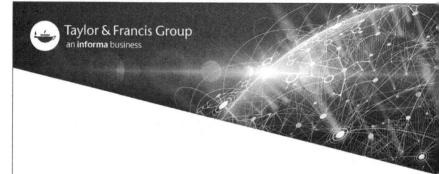

Printed in the United States
by Baker & Taylor Publisher Services